O.W.N YOUR SH!T

Your Inner 8-Year-Old Is Driving,
It's Time You Take the Wheel

Dr. Renee Brooks LPC-S

Dedication

To Kenneth,

For being both a witness and a participant in my growth, from a high school dropout to a Doctor of Psychology. Your unwavering patience, even when I didn't make it easy, and your steadfast support have been the foundation beneath me. I couldn't have done this without your belief in who I was becoming.

To my parents,

Thank you for never giving up on me and being exactly what I needed as parents.

To my clients,

You continue to trust me with your stories, and that trust has shaped me into the therapist I am today. Your courage to heal has inspired me, and for that, I am forever grateful.

And to God,

For keeping Your promise to use my pain for purpose.

What you're about to read will give you the tools to finally take your hands off the panic button and put them on the steering wheel. You will learn how your brain works when you're triggered. You will learn how your past plays out in your present. You will see the roots of your patterns and finally have the power to interrupt them.

Table of Contents

Introduction 1

Wake Up! 7

Chapter 1: The Good One 19

Gale's Story: Hijacked by the Wild Brain 20

The Hijacking Effect 21

Bringing the Observer Brain Online 23

Facts over Feelings 27

Chapter 2: Trapped in the Closet 35

Taylor's Story: Trapped in Survival Mode 37

Breaking the Cycle 38

Taylor's Transformation 42

Chapter 3: Rejected 47

Katie's Story – Desperate for Love 47

Katie's Wild Brain Takes Over 49

The Wild Brain in Full Force 49

The Roots of the Reaction 50

Breaking the Cycle 51

Finding Her Observer Brain 53

You're Not Alone 54

Chapter 4: The Fighter 59

Dave's Story: Defensive Instincts 59

The Incident that Broke it Open 60

The Bigger Picture 61

Breaking the Cycle 62

The Power Cycle: Changing the Narrative 64
Putting the Brakes on the Wild Brain 65
Moving Beyond the Pain 65

Chapter 5: The Blame Game 71
It's Never Just One Person 72
Stephanie's Story: Understanding the Emotional Hijack 73
Greg's Story: A Childhood Shaped by One Mistake 74
The Incident That Triggered the Crisis 74
The Wild Brain Takes Over 75
Breaking the Cycle 77
Moving Forward 77

Chapter 6: It's a Snake! 81
Brandy's Story: Life is a Battlefield 81
The Snake in the Park 82
The Wild Brain's Automatic Reaction 83
The Maladaptive Cycle 85
Getting the Observer Brain Back Online 85
Breaking Free from Phantom Snakes 87
Moving Forward 87

Chapter 7: Lie Vs the Irrefutable Truth 91
Emulu's Story: The Origin of the Lie 92
The Trap of Survival Mode 93
Paralyzed By the Lies 94
The Breakthrough 94
Breaking the Cycle 95
Embracing the Irrefutable Truth 95

Chapter 8: The Dance of Destruction 101
Hearing Voices from the Past 102
Dewayne's Story: The Roots of the Pain 102

Sophie's Story: Battles and Withdrawals 103
The Destructive Cycle 104
Breaking the Cycle 104
Shifting to the Power Cycle 107
The Importance of Regulation 110

Chapter 9: Emotionless 115
The Foundation Without the Glue 116
Kayla's Story: Childhood Conditioning 117
The Automatic Reaction: Laughter 118
Facing the Missing Pieces 118
Identifying the Core Feelings 119
Breaking the Cycle 119
Moving Forward 120

Chapter 10: The Intellect 125
Tasha's Story: The Perfect Family 126
Not Good Enough 127
The Agreement 128
When Silence Becomes Survival 128
The Relational Template 129
Awareness: Dating, Marriage, and Connection 131
Getting Out of Your Wounds and into Your Wisdom: The Irrefutable Truth 133
The Road to Change 134

Chapter 11: Own It 139
Seeing the Patterns in Yourself 140
The Three Brains: The Drivers Behind Your Behavior 140
The OWN Method: Observing What's Happening Now 141
The Feelings Cycle: Understanding Your Emotional Triggers 142

- The Power Cycle: Anchoring Yourself in Truth 142
- A Framework for Breaking the Cycle 143

Your Own Story 143
The Road Ahead 143
Final Words 144

Introduction

That's what the eight-year-old me was trained to do—attack first, defend always. I stood there stunned by what I had just said, unsure if I had finally gone too far. "I'm sorry," I whispered.

I stood in the kitchen, motionless. My feet felt nailed to the tile floor. I couldn't move. Couldn't speak. I just stared… at a brand-new jar of butter pickles.

My heart was heavy. Not from the pickles, of course, but from what they represented in that moment. Kenneth, my life partner, had just come home from work. Same cheerful pep in his step, same kiss on the cheek. But instead of following him into his man cave like I usually would, I stayed frozen in place, staring at that jar like it had betrayed me.

There was a war going on in my head. On one side was the rational adult me, saying, "Girl, it's not that deep. He didn't do anything wrong." But on the other side—the louder side—was the voice of my eight-year-old self, screaming, "He doesn't see you. You're invisible. You've always been invisible."

And just like that, I could feel it—my nervous system shifting. I was no longer in that present moment. I was in a familiar, wounded place. The disappointment hit fast and hard. I could feel the tears behind my eyes and the pressure building in my chest.

My thoughts were spiraling, and the urge to lash out—to make him feel what I was feeling—was so strong, it almost overtook me.

That's the thing about emotional triggers: they don't give you a warning.

Earlier that day, I'd been making Kenneth's favorite—tuna fish. Many years I've been making that damn tuna. It's our thing. It's simple, comforting, part of the rhythm of our lives. We were out of dill pickles, so I texted him and asked him to grab a jar on his way home. He replied, "Sure." So, I kept cooking, fully expecting the right pickles. But when I opened the grocery bag and saw butter pickles instead—something I never, ever use—I snapped internally.

In the grand scheme of life, it's not a big deal. But that moment wasn't about pickles. It was about being unseen. It was about eight-year-old me screaming that no one pays attention to what she needs, that her voice doesn't matter, that even the people closest to her never really *see* her.

If this had happened years ago, it would've ended in yelling. I would've made it his problem. Punished him with silence or sarcasm. Let the wounded child inside of me hijack the moment and turn it into a battlefield. But today—I didn't. I didn't lash out. I didn't weaponize my disappointment.

Instead, I took a deep breath and paused. I asked myself what part of me had just shown up—and why. I checked in with myself before I reacted. Because now, I know better. Now, I own it.

But I didn't always know how to do that.

Let me take you back.

It was years ago. Early in our relationship and before becoming a therapist. Kenneth and I were in the middle of what started as a simple disagreement. I don't even remember what the argument was about—something trivial. He hadn't done something fast enough for me, and before I knew it, I was shouting, "You can't do anything right!"

The words left my mouth like venom, and the moment they landed, I saw him deflate. I mean *deflate*. He stood there, shoulders sunk, pain all over his face. I was breathing hard, like I had just run a marathon, hands shaking, my eyes sharp with rage I couldn't explain.

I felt like I had to destroy something before it destroyed me. That's what the eight-year-old me was trained to do—attack first, defend always. I stood there stunned by what I had just said, unsure if I had finally gone too far. "I'm sorry," I whispered.

Twice. Once for him. Once for me.

That moment was my wake-up call.

I realized if I didn't do something—if I didn't figure out how to *own* what was happening inside me—I was going to ruin the very thing I loved most. I was going to keep ruining good things, good opportunities. I wasn't just carrying childhood baggage—I was unpacking it all over my relationship.

And it stunk.

That breakdown, and others like it, led me on a journey—not to find another coping technique or quick fix but to *understand* what was happening inside me. I needed to figure out how to stop letting my eight-year-old self run the show. How to stop putting that burden on Kenneth. Because let's be clear: It was never his job to raise my wounded inner child. That was *my* job.

My mission was to understand and share what I learned. Many years later, after becoming a therapist, my journey led me to study the brain. I dove into neuroscience. I traced my emotional reactions back to specific structures in the brain—the ones responsible for survival, memory, and reasoning. I realized my pain wasn't just emotional—it was *neurological.* And slowly, I began creating a method that I could use *in real time* to stop the spiral, regulate my nervous system, and respond instead of react.

That's how the OWN Method was born.

It's not a theory. It's not a buzzword. It's a process—a simple, practical, powerful process—that teaches you how to *Own* what you feel, *Work through* what it means, and *Name* a new response. It's how you go from triggered and toxic to calm and clear. It's how you stop waiting for someone else to fix you and start regulating yourself.

This book isn't here to coddle you. It's here to wake you up.

If you've ever found yourself lashing out and then regretting it... If you've ever ruined a moment, a relationship, or an opportunity because your inner child took the wheel... If you feel like you're always stuck in the same emotional loops, reacting before you even realize what you're reacting to, then this book is for you.

What you're about to read will give you the tools to finally take your hands off the panic button and put them on the steering wheel. You will learn how your brain works when you're triggered. You will learn how your past plays out in your present. You will see the roots of your patterns and finally have the power to interrupt them.

You're not broken. You're patterned.

And those patterns can be rewired.

"How will this book benefit me?" you ask.

It'll teach you how to stop letting your childhood write your adult story. It'll show you how to stop reacting from wounds and start responding from wisdom. It'll give you the tools to regulate yourself—so you stop expecting other people to carry what's yours to carry. It'll help you clean up your emotional mess before it stinks up your life, your love, your career, your peace.

This book is your mirror, your permission slip, and *your* **wake-up call.**

If you're courageous enough, let's get started.

What did you have to become to survive your childhood?

Wake Up!

Who are you when your emotional triggers get activated?

As a psychotherapist, I sit with individuals daily who are completely unaware of the baggage they carry. Most of my clients seek out therapy only after a major relationship has fallen apart— a romantic relationship, a friendship, or even a business partnership. When these significant relationships crash and burn, people start looking for answers, especially if it seems like *every* relationship ends in the same, predictable way. *Is it me? Why do my relationships always end like this? Am I not good enough? Why am I the only one single? Why is everyone else's business or career thriving? Shouldn't I be further than this in my life?* I've heard these questions over and over again. Day after day, I watch individuals feel hopeless, anxious, and drained as they sit on my couch, desperate for a solution.

These questions can feel impossible to answer—especially if you can't quite pinpoint what's going wrong. And that makes sense, because you *don't* experience yourself from the outside. You have no idea what it's actually like for someone else to attempt to build a relationship with you. You have no idea what it feels like to connect with your invisible baggage. From your perspective, you probably feel like you're easy to deal with, compassionate, reasonable—maybe even an ideal partner. So, it's tempting to think, *It's not me. I'm a good person, I try to love and care for others, so it must be them.*

And you could be right. You *could* be a genuinely loving, caring, and wonderful person. But even so, it could still be extremely difficult for others to connect with you. Why? Because of your baggage—who you are at a much *deeper* level. Not who you are on the surface but who you are when your emotional triggers get activated, when your baggage hijacks your reactions, and when those subtle (but powerful) survival strategies you learned as a child start to run the show.

Out of sight out of mind, right? If we don't see it, we assume it doesn't exist. It sits at the very core of who we are, buried so deep that we're not even aware it's there, and yet it's running our lives. It's the stuff that's secretly anchored itself in the deepest parts of you without you even knowing it. It's like the imaginary friend who helped you get through childhood but turned on you in adulthood. Childhood baggage is a set of survival tactics that were effective when you were a kid but have become toxic in your adult life.

The issue with childhood baggage is that it's hard to pinpoint. It shows up in our lives automatically. It's sneaky and subtle, causing us to behave on autopilot, react without thinking, and sabotage our relationships before we even realize what's happening. Most of us have no idea when it shows up, how it influences us, or how it has us repeating the same patterns, relationship after relationship.

Ignorance in this area only becomes a pathway to blaming others and constantly seeking reasons outside of ourselves for why we are single, divorced, or stuck in life. I've heard them all: *The reason this relationship didn't work is because I couldn't hold her accountable. He's not emotionally intelligent enough. She's not feminine enough. He's too sassy. She has nothing to bring to the table. Men are intimidated by my strength.* All examples of outward thinking that will only lead you back to being stuck, lonely, and unsuccessful.

The problem is as long as we seek outside of ourselves for cause, the baggage remains hidden, festering under the radar, ready to strike—again.

So, here we go. Let's wake it up now with one simple question: **What did you have to become to survive your childhood?**

Think about it. To survive whatever environment you grew up in—whether that was chaotic, neglectful, overly critical, or simply emotionally unavailable—what did you have to turn into? Did you have to:

- Turn off your emotions to deal with an unavailable parent?
- Become the "responsible one" to clean up after a parent who was an addict?
- Strive for perfection to avoid the wrath of judgmental, critical parents?
- Withdraw into yourself to survive abusive caregivers?
- Or did you have to become the "Good one" because your siblings demanded all of your parents' attention?

Now, think even deeper: **What beliefs did you create about yourself as you were just trying to survive?**

- "I'm not important."
- "I have to be perfect to be loved."
- "I can't ever make mistakes."

- "I'm not lovable."
- "I'm not safe because people will always hurt me."

And let's talk about how you reacted to those beliefs:

- Did you shut down and go silent, convinced no one would care?
- Did you lash out at the slightest hint of rejection?
- Did you become hyper-vigilant, constantly scanning other people's behaviors to protect yourself?
- Did you learn to fake being perfect, never allowing yourself to show weakness or need?

Whatever you had to become, whatever thoughts, feelings, and reactions you took on were necessary for survival back then. But now, they're poisoning your adult life. The survival mechanisms that kept you safe as a child are screwing up your relationships today.

So, here's the deal: It's not your fault that these things happened to you. But it *is* your responsibility to fix it. Why? Because if you don't, your baggage is going to keep owning you, your life, and your relationships. It's going to keep stinking up your world.

Unlike trauma, we *all* have baggage. But here's the thing—nobody wants to carry yours. You can't expect others to deal with your childish thoughts, your defensiveness, your outbursts, your insecurities. No one wants to sign up for managing their own baggage *and* yours. So, stop expecting it.

Sh!t is sh!t. You can't give it away, and you can't hide it. What you can—and *must*—do with it is *own it*. Because it belongs to you.

When baggage goes unattended, it starts to stink. And you can't dress it up. You can't wrap it in a designer suit or slap on some fancy perfume. Sh!t is sh!t. You can't give it away, and you can't hide it. What you can—and *must*—do with it is *own it*. Because it belongs to you.

Refuse to own it, and you'll keep finding yourself in the same painful cycles over and over.

So, what does owning it mean?

It means becoming aware of it. It means learning to identify the feelings, thoughts, and reactions that push people away or cause conflict. It means choosing new behaviors that will actually get you what you want instead of the same old shitshow.

But first, you have to understand how this baggage found its way into your adult life. Science is clear that our most emotionally intense experiences from childhood are stored in our bodies—they never go away. It's all stored in your brain; the midbrain, to be exact. So, let's take a look at the three parts of the brain that play a role in storing these experiences. While the brain is much more complex, I have oversimplified and nicknamed parts of the brain to keep it simple.

The Three Brains:

1. **The Newborn Brain (Reptilian)**: The brain is built from the bottom up. The first part of the brain is created while still in the womb. This is the automatic part of the brain, concerned only with immediate survival through reflexive behaviors.
2. **The Wild Brain (Midbrain)**: After birth, we develop the midbrain, which I call the "wild brain." This is where

all your baggage is stored, where your eight-year-old self resides. This is where the sh!t is stored—the experiences from ages birth to twenty-five. The wild brain does a great job of recording memories but lacks the ability to analyze and interpret situations correctly. It only has experiences and the narratives we create about those experiences. The problem is most of the narratives stored in your wild brain were created by a much younger version of you—a version that didn't yet have the insight, intellect, or life experience to tell the full truth about what was happening. That means these old stories are often distorted, outdated, and incomplete. And when your wild brain gets activated, it doesn't stop to fact-check—it just reacts. It pulls in the newborn brain to help it survive, and together, they make up the emotional brain. This emotional brain houses your limbic system—the part of your nervous system that runs on survival. It doesn't analyze. It doesn't reflect. It only knows how to fight, flee, or fawn.

3. **The Observer Brain (Neocortex)**: After twenty-five, we develop the adult brain, which I call the "observer brain." This part has the ability to tell us the truth about experiences, even those stored in our wild brain. It observes, analyzes, and interprets situations, offering us not a made-up narrative but the facts. This explains why we act less recklessly as we age.

We're going to spend a lot of time talking about the wild brain in this book—for good reason. That's the part of your brain that keeps causing problems. It's where the chaos starts. The wild thoughts, the overreactions, the emotional spirals, the destructive behaviors—it's all coming from there.

This part of the brain is called the limbic system. It houses the amygdala, which is basically your brain's smoke alarm. The second it thinks something feels threatening—emotionally or physically—it sounds the alarm and throws you straight into survival mode. And when survival mode kicks in, guess who shows up?

The eight-year-old version of you.

That wounded child inside of you—the one who never felt safe, never felt heard, who learned to survive however they could—they wake up and start running the show. That part of you doesn't care that you're an adult now. It doesn't stop to assess reality. It just reacts. Loudly. Desperately. Without thinking.

I've lived this. I talk about it in the story of the damn butter pickles. I stood in the kitchen, shaking with anger, not because of pickles but because the eight-year-old in me had been triggered. She was screaming at me—"See, you're not important! They never think about you! Leave! Protect yourself!" She didn't care that I was in a loving relationship or that I had tools to regulate. She wanted out. That's what the wild brain does—it floods you with the same panic and hurt you felt when you were too young to make sense of what was happening.

That's why we're starting here. Because if you don't understand how your wild brain works—and more importantly, how to calm it down—you'll keep getting hijacked by it. You'll keep letting your eight-year-old self react to grown-up situations with outdated survival strategies. That's how we destroy relationships, self-sabotage, shut down, or lash out—and we don't even realize it's happening.

This is where the "OWN Method" comes in. OWN is a reminder to stop and Observe What's happening Now (OWN)! It's a straightforward approach that will help you break the destructive cycle you may find yourself in today. The OWN Method will help you become aware of your baggage, identify it, and ultimately own it so that it stops owning you.

1

"Just because your survival didn't look like chaos doesn't mean it wasn't costly."

-Dr. Renee

"Have you ever considered that maybe you are what's holding you back?"

Chapter One

The Good One

Gale was becoming frustrated with herself. She was constantly being passed over at work. When promotions were handed out, she was overlooked year after year. She would sit quietly in her office, wondering why she wasn't good enough to receive a promotion. She reported to me that she often felt forgettable and ***"left out."***

"I've gone through this all my life. As a little girl, I was left out because **I was too dark**. When I got older, **I was too tall** to date. Now, it's happening again."

Gale was now in her forties and still being **"looked over"** at work and in her dating life.

"Even when I date, I'm always being told what a great person I am, how I would be a great wife, **but they never choose me. They always choose someone else."**

On a surface level, it would be easy to assume that Gale was just running into a lot of unfortunate situations. She was highly intelligent—a beautiful African American woman who was softspoken and always ready to offer help to anyone who needed it. But year after year, she was finding herself in the same situations: single and stuck in the same position at work. Gale used the same behaviors when dating. She would stay quiet about her true desires to be in a committed relationships due to the fear that she would run the men away. Instead of speaking up, she would either position herself as a helpful friend who was always available to listen, or she would shrink down and just hope they read her mind.

"Gale," I asked, taking a sip of my tea, "have you ever considered that maybe you are what's holding you back?" Gale immediately looked down at her hands. I knew it was important to wake her up to her behaviors and get to the core of the issues she continued to experience. Allowing her to express how she felt "looked over" was one thing: however, getting to the core of her sh!t that has been lying dormant in her life and driving her behaviors was the key. So, let's do some digging.

Gale's Story: Hijacked by the Wild Brain

Gale was the oldest in her family. She was deemed the ***"responsible one."*** *The one who would always do good, never rock the boat, kept her head down, and worked hard to reach her parents' expectations of her. Her other siblings were the "troublemakers"—the ones her parents had to devote their undivided attention to. Gale was also responsible for helping her siblings stay out of trouble. She was rewarded with words of affirmation for being the "good one."* ***Her parents would often say, "We don't have to worry about you.*** *We know you will never give us problems, and you even help us with your siblings. You're such a great daughter."*

While this seemed harmless, it set a quiet expectation for Gale and left no room for her to express the isolation and emotional abandonment she experienced growing up. She often felt pushed aside and alone but kept it all to herself. She pretended to be content so that she didn't become another problem child for her parents.

This is what it looked like for Gale:

- **Wild Brain:** It's easy to forget about you. You just need to keep your head down and your mouth closed. Everyone else is more important than you. You don't have the right to express yourself, because if you do, you will cause problems. **Your value is your ability to stay out of the way.**
- **Newborn Brain:** Isolate yourself. Shut down, say nothing.

The Hijacking Effect

When your wild brain takes control, it hijacks your entire system. It's like putting a teenager behind the wheel of a car—they're impulsive, emotional, and don't think through the consequences of their actions. The wild brain does the same thing. It reacts without thinking, based on the old stories and traumas stored deep inside.

And because the wild brain can't differentiate between past and present, it reacts to today's situations as if you're still living in your childhood, stuck in survival mode. Moreover, if we aren't careful, we will inadvertently set our life up as if we are still surviving one of those childhood experiences, just as Gale had done.

Ever notice how you react out of proportion to something small? Like lashing out at your partner for not texting you back, or feeling abandoned the second someone doesn't respond the way you expect? That's your wild brain, pulling from old, stored pain and turning every situation into a fight for survival. It's convinced you're under attack, when really, you're not. When the wild brain is activated, if you pay close enough attention, you will notice the physical symptoms. Symptoms such as chest tightening, racing heart, or overall tense body, rubbing your hands together, or clenched jaw—just to name a few.

Without even knowing it, Gale was still isolating herself and staying quiet because she didn't want to cause problems, but her staying quiet now had become the problem. The very action she took to successfully survive her childhood now had become a wall separating her from what she truly desired. Gale and I were able to identify how her wild brain was driving the vehicle of her life.

It wasn't that she was overlooked due to her being too dark, too tall, or that she lacked skill. Gale was overlooked because she pretended to be content in her current role to ensure that she didn't cause problems at work. She shrunk herself to avoid issues, all the while desiring to be seen and promoted. Gale was able to identify how her feelings, thoughts, and actions from her childhood were hijacking her and keeping her stuck in survival mode at work, which resulted in stagnation within the company.

She had been convinced that she was once again in a situation where the expectation of her was to sit back and be the **"good one."** Gale was, in essence, stuck in survival mode without knowing it—constantly believing she would only cause problems if she spoke up for herself. In order to survive at work, she isolated, put her head down, and pretended to be content.

Gale's survival strategy looked nothing like mine—but it was survival all the same. When my eight-year-old self was triggered, she came out swinging. She yelled, demanded, and made sure everyone knew she was upset. Gale's eight-year-old didn't yell—she hid. Hers was the quieter kind of survival but just as destructive. Instead of creating conflict, she avoided it at all costs. While my wounded child demanded to be seen, hers convinced her it was safer to disappear. But the result was the same: both of us were being driven by outdated strategies from childhood. Where I fought, Gale retreated. Where I lashed out, she shut down. But both of us were being hijacked by children who no longer needed to be in charge. That's why this work matters—because whether your wounded child fights or flees, if you don't learn to recognize who's driving, you'll keep ending up in places you don't want to be.

This is why regulation is non-negotiable. When your wild brain is activated, the observer brain—the one that sees clearly, that helps you choose wisely—goes offline. The two can't operate at the same time. They're anticorrelated, meaning when one is active, the other is quiet. That's why it's so crucial to calm yourself down when you're triggered. You need to create enough space between the feeling and the reaction for the observer brain to come back online. Without it, you're stuck in survival mode, reacting with old behaviors that no longer serve you. But when you learn to pause, breathe, and OWN the moment—you stop surviving and start choosing. That's when everything changes.

Bringing the Observer Brain Online

So, how do you stop the cycle? You bring your observer brain online—and that's where the OWN Method comes in.

The OWN Method gives you a simple, practical way to interrupt your automatic reactions and regain control. Instead of letting your wounded, wild brain run the show, you pause, check in, and choose a better response.

It starts by asking yourself three questions in the heat of the moment:

- What am I feeling?
- What are my thoughts?
- How do I typically react when I feel this way?

These questions give your observer brain—the calm, logical part of your mind—a chance to step up and take the wheel. Once you identify the emotion (fear, sadness, anger), connect it to the thought driving it ("I'm not safe," "I'm not wanted," "I'm going to be abandoned"), and recognize the behavior that usually follows (yelling, withdrawing, chasing, avoiding).

You're no longer being hijacked by your past, you're calming the eight-year-old. You're assuring them that you've got it now.

You're moving from automatic reaction to intentional response.

You're choosing awareness.

You're choosing growth.

You're choosing to OWN it.

Now, here's the truth that saves many relationships: Don't attempt to have any conversations until you've answered all three questions. If you do, your eight-year-old wounded self will be doing the talking—and that's almost always a disaster. Why? Because you haven't taken enough time to figure out what's really going on inside you. You may think you're angry, but after checking in, you realize you're actually disappointed, hurt, or scared. And if you don't know what you're truly feeling, how can anyone else?

Worse, when you're dysregulated and start yelling or reacting, the other person usually stops listening. They're no longer hearing your words—they're watching your body language, bracing for impact, and planning their defense. That conversation you needed to go well? It just turned into a battlefield.

No important decisions or conversations should happen before you've done this work. Period. The OWN Method helps you regulate first, then speak from a place of clarity. That makes all the difference. When you're able to clearly express how you truly feel, people can finally hear you—and connection becomes possible again.

And let's not forget this part—your partner has an eight-year-old too. If you try to have a conversation while you're dysregulated, now you've got two wounded children at the table—both flooded with feelings, overwhelmed with thoughts, and trying to escape the discomfort. This is exactly what I see in my office too often. And over time, what happens is predictable: The relationship becomes an environment neither of you can survive in. Someone shuts down, someone checks out, and eventually, the relationship becomes a place both people abandon—whether it's through divorce, infidelity, or emotional detachment.

Here's what I know for sure: You don't want to create a relationship your partner has to *survive*. If you do, I can almost guarantee—you'll end up regretting it.

Gale and I spent several sessions identifying her core thoughts and feelings when she was triggered by utilizing the three questions. In order for Gale to become aware of her core triggering feelings and emotions, we created the chart below.

First, let's make sure you understand how to utilize the three crucial questions.

What do I feel?

Start by naming the primary emotion you're experiencing. If you can't find the right word, use a feelings wheel to narrow it down. Are you really angry or are you actually feeling hurt, disappointed, or betrayed?

What are my thoughts?

Identify the thoughts that automatically follow your feelings.

When you're upset, what's your wild brain saying to you? Is it screaming, "You're not good enough" or "They're out to get you"?

What are my typical actions or reactions?

Look at how you usually behave when these thoughts and feelings take over—those knee-jerk reactions. Do you lash out, shut down, or retreat? Identifying these automatic reactions is crucial to breaking the cycle.

Gale's Chart

Feelings	Thoughts	Actions
Rejected	I'm too tall. I'm too dark	Exclude myself
Unimportant	Other people are more important than I am	Shrink down
Lonely	I'm not good enough	Isolate
Worried	Speaking up will cause problems	Shut down

She thought being a quiet, intelligent, helpful employee would one day get her seen; she soon realized that was never going to happen. Her shrinking down was causing her to be invisible—if you will—thus making it easy to forget her or even look over her. Initially, Gale was frustrated because she was being looked over, which didn't make sense to her given she was such a nice person. However, when she was able to label her real feelings, she was able to see that feeling rejected threw her into her familiar cycle of shrinking and saying nothing; in essence, she regressed back to being "the good one."

Facts over Feelings

Once you've paused long enough to ask yourself the first three questions, you've started the process of pulling yourself out of survival mode. But self-awareness alone isn't enough. You need a new path forward. This is where the second part of the OWN Method kicks in and gives you something most people never had growing up: tools to anchor yourself in truth rather than fear.

When the wild brain is triggered, it lies. It pulls from old, outdated memories and convinces you that what's happening now is just like what happened then. The goal of this next step is to anchor yourself in the present and replace the survival story with reality. You do that by asking yourself three more questions:

1. What do I know?
2. What is the irrefutable truth?
3. What will the new action be?

Let me walk you through how this looked for me.

In the pickle story I shared earlier, I was activated. It felt like Kenneth had dismissed me, ignored what I'd said about what

I liked, and made a decision that didn't include me. My eight-year-old self was screaming, "He doesn't see you. You're invisible again. You're not valued." That child inside me was hurt—and ready to fight.

But I didn't let her take the wheel. I stopped. I breathed. And I answered those three questions.

What do I know? I know Kenneth has consistently shown up for me. For many years, he has proven in countless ways that he loves and values me.

What is the irrefutable truth? The truth is, Kenneth wasn't trying to dismiss me. In fact, he thought I'd like to try something new because he knows I enjoy experimenting with flavors and recipes.

What will the new action be? I chose to regulate myself first. Then I calmly asked him why he chose those pickles. And once he explained, I completely understood.

The conversation went smoothly—because I did my work first.

This isn't a one-time fix. Regulation is a practice. You have to do it over and over again. It's not automatic at first, but if you keep at it, it becomes easier. You build new patterns. New defaults. New wiring.

That's the power of the OWN Method—it gives you real, tangible steps to calm the wounded child, deactivate the wild brain, and bring the observer brain back online. You stop reacting from old pain and start responding from present truth.

Science backs this up. In *The Body Keeps the Score*, Bessel van der Kolk explains that the brain is not fixed—it's adaptable. This concept, known as **neuroplasticity**, means your brain can rewire itself based on repeated experiences. When you consistently interrupt your old automatic reactions and practice new ways of thinking, feeling, and responding, you're literally training your brain to build new pathways. Over time, the wild brain's knee-jerk responses get weaker, and the observer brain becomes stronger and more accessible.

But the key word is **practice**. Regulation doesn't become your default overnight. You have to do it over and over again—until the new way becomes the familiar way. And that's exactly what the OWN Method is designed to help you do: interrupt old survival cycles and create new, regulated ones that align with the truth of who you are today—not the fears of who you used to be.

Gale learned to utilize the next three sets of questions to help her move from the midbrain, which continued to confirm her shrinking down, to her observer brain, which allowed her to interpret the situation accurately.

Gale was eventually able to break that cycle by identifying what she **knew** versus how she **felt**. She was able to access the irrefutable truth about herself, and lastly, she became intentional about not sitting back and being quiet. Rather, she spoke up for herself and asked for what she wanted.

This is a crucial part of the steps in that the ability to discover what you know for sure about the situation has the potential to pull you out of survival mode instantaneously.

Gale's Chart

What I Know	The Irrefutable Truth	The new action
I have no clear evidence that someone is rejecting me	I've only heard great things about myself. My co-workers continue to come to me for my advice and help because they admire and trust me.	I will make sure my organization understands that I'm ready and fully prepared to offer more of what I've always offered.
I'm important to my company	I've been successful for many years at this corporation, and I'm constantly given kudos and accolades for my work.	I will give myself the credit I deserve, and I will speak with confidence when asking for promotions, knowing that I've already proven myself.
Staying quiet is not helping me	I've been quiet for years, pretending I was content, and that only led to more years of the same old thing.	I will speak up and let my corporation know that I'm highly skilled and ready to advance.

I have great character traits that most men enjoy and find highly attractive.	I've refused to speak up about what I wanted in relationships, and most men looked over me as someone who desired a committed relationship.	I will speak up about my desire to be in a committed relationship. When dating, I will use my voice, I will not pretend I'm okay with being the "go-to" friend.

Gale has not only received a huge promotion; she is now preparing to become one of the first African American vice presidents of her company.

Gale is the epitome of someone who wouldn't consider her childhood traumatic; however, the baggage from her childhood was running rampant, until she learned to identify it, own it, and change it. When you can do this—when you can pause, identify what's really happening, and bring your observer brain online—you take back control. You get to choose how you respond, instead of letting your wild brain run the show.

Let's go deeper.

QUESTION

"Have you ever found yourself playing the 'good one' role, hoping it would be enough to get noticed, valued, or chosen? What parts of yourself have you been holding back in the hope of keeping the peace—and what might happen if you allowed yourself to be seen, fully?"

2

“Survival that taught you to fight will convince you that peace is weakness.”

-Dr. Renee

Most of us run on autopilot when we're triggered. We react without even realizing what's happening, and before we know it, we're deep in behavior that keeps us stuck.

Chapter Two

Trapped in the Closet

Taylor was angry. It was clear she felt trapped, with no other option but to fight. The moment she walked into my office, she looked at me and said, "I'm probably going to jail today." Taylor had experienced a series of difficult events—she'd recently lost her godson, a lifelong friendship had ended, and her long-term romantic relationship was crumbling. She was barely holding it together, and this day, she was reaching her breaking point.

"I'm about to do something that I'll later regret," she explained.

Taylor was very aware that she was triggered, and she also knew she was a fighter. Her awareness was a good start, but knowing she was triggered wasn't enough to stop what was happening inside her. Taylor was already at the edge, and every situation she encountered at work felt magnified.

"I'm tired of people thinking they can take advantage of me," she said. **"I'm done letting people treat me like I'm nothing."**

That day, she saw a co-worker mistreating a patient, and she lost it. Taylor explained that she absolutely had zero tolerance for her colleagues mistreating the patients. But when she spoke about it, she was trembling with more than just anger. She also felt betrayed and exhausted. It wasn't just about the patients or the job—it was about everything.

Taylor went on to talk about how she felt used and betrayed by her best friend. She also shared how her partner expected her to handle everything.

"I'm the only one working. He's struggling with his own mental health, but it's like I'm supposed to just keep carrying all of it. I feel like he's taking advantage of me at this point."

Taylor hadn't realized it yet, but she was surviving her relationship and doing the only things she knew to do to feel valuable. While she had grown tired of supporting her boyfriend, she didn't dare stop because she feared he would leave—leaving her alone and feeling worthless. She was in essence using the only tool she had to feel valuable: giving of herself until she was completely empty.

Taylor had been the breadwinner for years, but now she was tired—**tired of carrying everyone and everything**. She continued to insist, "I don't care anymore," but it was obvious she did care. Maybe she cared too much.

It was clear that Taylor's wild brain was running the show. I knew it would be vital to provide her with tools to get her out of her wild brain and into her observing brain before she did something she would regret.

"Taylor," I said calmly, "you have spent an hour telling me how much the younger you had to endure. I don't think it's fair that the adult you wants to act out of impulse and do something reckless that's going to result in her sitting in jail, I think you owe her more than that."

Taylor immediately calmed down and sat back on the couch with her eyes still locked with mine.

Taylor's Story: Trapped in Survival Mode

"She would fill my ears with music so I didn't hear what was going on outside."

Taylor's voice softened as she began to explain how her older sister tried to protect her from the chaos at home by pushing her into their bedroom closet when their parents would fight. "I always knew what was going on, but she would push me into a closet and put the earphones over my ears anyway."

Taylor recalled watching her parents abuse each other for years.

Her mom would throw her dad out, swear she wouldn't let him back in, only to break that promise a few weeks later. As the youngest child, Taylor found herself in the middle of the fights, running out of the closet to stand between her parents. She tried to fight her dad, to protect her mom, but nothing ever changed.

"I just remember being trapped in that closet, feeling angry and ready to fight."

But the anger wasn't just directed at her father. Some of her rage turned toward her mom for staying with him, for creating that environment, for making promises she never kept. She felt betrayed and abandoned in that closet.

"It seems like everything I go through in life takes me back to being in that damn closet," she said.

Taylor had experienced major losses—her godson, her friend, the end of relationships—and each time, it felt like she was that little girl: stuck, powerless, and enraged.

"I should have been dead," Taylor explained. She began listing off the times she'd almost died—being run over by a car, a severe accident as a child. She'd been assaulted by a family member on several occasions, and yet she kept pushing through.

"I've gone through so much. I don't even know how I survived."

Taylor dwelled in her pain without even realizing it. She was a fighter, yes, but all those battles—both external and internal—were fueled by an old story her wild brain had kept alive for decades.

Breaking the Cycle

Over a few sessions, I taught Taylor to stop and Observe What's happening Now, which she renamed "the sister girl check in." She started to learn how to become mindful of what her body was doing when she felt triggered; but also, she learned to utilize both sets of questions to shift from being on autopilot to being more mindfully aware of what was happening.

As we explored in the previous chapter, we used a chart—but we didn't stop there. We pulled in other tools too, all designed to help her connect the dots between her feelings, thoughts, and the destructive cycles they kept feeding.

Most of us run on autopilot when we're triggered. We react without even realizing what's happening, and before we know it, we're deep in behavior that keeps us stuck. That's why learning your pattern matters. When you can see the cycle clearly—what you feel, what you think, how you react—you're in a better position to interrupt it. Awareness gives you the chance to get ahead of it, to pause before you say or do something you'll wish you hadn't. That's the power of owning it.

I introduced Taylor to the **Feelings Cycle** and the **Power Cycle**—two practical tools designed to help her identify her triggers, understand her automatic reactions, and replace them with intentional responses.

The **Feelings Cycle** helped Taylor become aware of her emotional patterns by breaking down what happens inside her when she's triggered. We started by identifying what she felt, moved into the thoughts that accompanied those feelings, and then highlighted her automatic actions. By mapping out her typical responses, Taylor gained clarity on how her childhood experiences were still showing up in her adult life.

Taylor was able to identify (using a feelings wheel) that she wasn't just angry—she felt **betrayed** and **powerless**. Betrayed by a mother who kept allowing her abusive father back into their lives. Powerless because no matter how hard she tried to protect her mom, it was never enough. As a little girl, sitting in that closet, she vowed to never feel powerless again. She promised herself she would always fight back. So, any time someone dared to make her feel helpless or if she found even the smallest evidence that someone was trying to take advantage of her, she would "fight to the death."

Here's what Taylor's **Feelings Cycle** looked like:

- **Feelings:** Betrayed and powerless
- **Thoughts:** People will hurt me or take advantage of me if I don't fight
- **Action:** Physically fight or lash out verbally

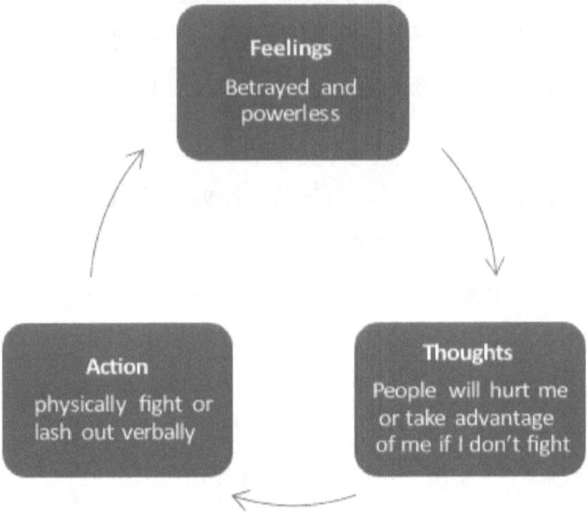

Feelings cycle

Taylor was a fighter—that much was obvious. But what she didn't know was the thoughts and feelings that drove her into fighting. Now she could see that her wild brain was always playing in the background, telling her to fight because someone was either taking advantage of her or trying to render her powerless. Taylor could also see how her thoughts and actions only landed her back in the same feelings over and over again.

Taylor's wild brain was also triggered at work when she thought a patient was being mistreated. She had been conditioned to fight for others, just like she did as a young girl. Although her sister would try to trap her in the closet, Taylor would always find her way around her sister—out of the closet and in between her brawling parents.

Then, we flipped the script with the **Power Cycle**. The Power Cycle is more than just a tool—it's a visual of what it looks like when you're standing in your power. While the Feelings Cycle shows what happens when you're dysregulated and your eight-year-old self is behind the wheel, the Power Cycle represents the moment your adult self takes the wheel and chooses a different route. It's what happens when you stop letting your wild brain write the narrative and start anchoring yourself in truth. Using the Power Cycle helps you break the destructive loop by showing how to create a new one—one grounded in awareness, clarity, and choice. It's the shift from survival to intentional living. It's what it looks like when you stop reacting from old pain and start responding from present truth. This is what it means to truly *own your sh!t.*

- **What I Know:** I know how to take care of myself.

  Not everyone is trying to hurt me. I'm not powerless. My mom's decisions were based on what she knew at that time; she never intended to betray me. I'm a good person, and I deserve to be with people who value me and my effort. My value is not dependent upon my setting myself on fire to keep other people warm. I have a very powerful voice, so I don't need to fight or get loud to protect myself or others. I know how to leave situations that are harmful to me.

- **Irrefutable Truth:** I have endured a lot of loss in my life, but I kept overcoming it with God's help. He has always and will always protect me. I have been successful at taking care of myself; at times, without fighting or lashing out. My power is what I pulled from to complete my education, even while going through a lot at home—I am powerful.

- **Action:** I will talk things out with people when I feel it is necessary, or I will disconnect from people who do not see the value in me or are harmful to me. I will protect myself and others through effective communication.

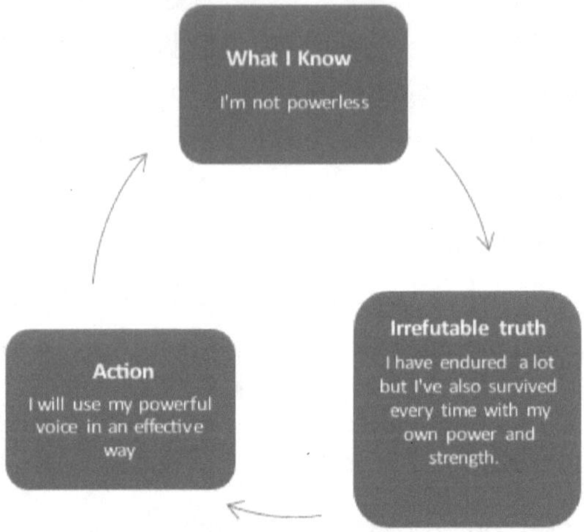

Power Cycle

Taylor's Transformation

Today, Taylor's family and friends constantly tell her how inspired they are by the changes she has made. She no longer lashes out, although she still doesn't shy away from a challenging conversation or conflict. Taylor decided to leave her boyfriend of more than ten years. She also began to express to her mother all the times she felt let down, and the conversations, while emotionally intense, have not escalated into fights as they had in the past.

Taylor continues to work at the same place, where even her coworkers have noticed a huge shift in her.

And most of all, Taylor never went to jail, and that was the goal.

Let's go deeper.

QUESTION

Have you ever felt like you're fighting the same battles and overreacting to people and situations as if you're still that younger version of yourself, stuck in survival mode?

3

"You're not needy. You're still asking for what you never got— *but expecting someone else to fix it will break everything."*

-Dr. Renee

Someone who's insecure demanding their mate do something or stop doing something because they are insecure. Not only does that not work, it's unfair, out of order, and destructive. The sh!t from your past that causes you to feel insecure is yours to own, not your mate's.

Chapter Three

Rejected

Katie sat in my office, her eyes red from sleepless nights and endless tears. She was on the brink of losing her third marriage, and she couldn't understand why. ***"I feel uncared for, unsupported, rejected, and abandoned*** *all over again," she whispered. Katie's eyes were empty and dark. She continued to speak as if she had gotten lost in her own thoughts. She didn't blink. She didn't move her body. She was frozen—possibly paralyzed by the stories her wild brain was whispering to her. Katie and I sat in silence as I watched her fall deeper into herself.*

"This is why I don't trust anyone," *she said, finally breaking the silence. "****Why does this keep happening to me****?"*

"Katie," I said, determined to get her to see some reality, "if this is the third marriage, and the other two ended the exact same way, I'd like you to focus more on the common denominator and less on the outcome."

Katie's Story – Desperate for Love

Katie's childhood was marked by chaos and instability. By age seven, she had been yanked out of her home because both of her parents were addicts. She bounced from one family member's house to another, each stop seemingly worse than the last. Abuse was a constant companion—verbal, emotional, even sexual. The one time she mustered the courage to tell an adult about what was happening, she was blamed and thrown out of the house. Treated like an unwelcome guest, she was never given the love, care, or compassion that the other children in the household received. Katie was a burden—tolerated but never truly embraced.

By the time she entered high school, Katie was left to fend for herself. No financial support, no lunch money, no guidance. She buried herself in schoolwork, excelling in every class as a way to escape her grim reality. But no matter how well she did, the feelings of being unsafe, uncared for, abandoned, and rejected clung to her like a shadow, seeping into every corner of her life.

Then she met him—a young man who showed her the attention she so desperately craved. He was loving and caring, everything she'd been starved of her whole life. They wasted no time; they dated and got married as soon as they graduated. Katie thought she'd finally found her safe haven with him. This would be her first marriage, which lasted only three short years. Katie explained that although he was able to provide the emotional attention she desired, she would often feel uncared for and unsafe. Katie divorced her first husband and quickly remarried. The second marriage started and ended quite the same. After a few short years, she found herself feeling unlovable and unsafe, which resulted in her leaving the marriage—again. Katie had become an expert at gathering the evidence she needed to confirm that she was **unlovable, unimportant, and not worthy of love**. She was so caught up in feeling rejected that she couldn't see the obvious.

Katie's Wild Brain Takes Over

As we continued our sessions, it became clear that the real problem wasn't what was happening *to* Katie—it was how she was perceiving it. Her wild brain was hijacking her thoughts and reactions. The deep-seated beliefs and narratives it carried were shaped by years of instability, rejection, and neglect. This wasn't just a "personality flaw" or a "bad habit." Katie's wild brain had been running the show for so long that she couldn't see it for what it was.

We traced it back to her childhood experiences, which had burned certain messages into her wild brain. For Katie, these messages were something like:

- "You're not safe."
- "People will hurt you."
- "No one cares about you."
- "You'll always be alone."

These thoughts didn't just fade away because she grew up. The wild brain recorded them like a broken record, playing them over and over. Whenever something triggered a memory—like being left out, feeling ignored, or seeing her husband's group text that included other women—her wild brain jumped into action.

The Wild Brain in Full Force

One day, during our session, Katie described a typical situation that would set her off.

Her husband had texted a few people from work in a group chat. Katie had seen the message and felt the familiar pang of insecurity.

"Are there women in this group?" she asked him.

When he admitted there were both men and women, she exploded.

"You know I'm insecure! You know I don't feel safe! Why would you do this to me?"

Her husband, blindsided, tried to explain. He said it was just a polite message to some of his co-workers—nothing more. But by that time, her wild brain had taken over. It screamed, "**You're not safe! He's going to leave you! Protect yourself!**" And Katie lashed out—not based on the reality of the situation but on the emotional narrative stored deep within her wild brain.

This cycle of suspicion, rage, and lashing out wasn't new. It had been there in every one of her marriages. Her wild brain was convinced that it was protecting her. But it wasn't. It was destroying everything. This is a common issue I see as a clinician. Someone who's insecure demanding their mate do something or stop doing something because they are insecure. Not only does that not work, it's unfair, out of order, and destructive. The sh!t from your past that causes you to feel insecure is yours to own, not your mate's. If you continue to try and put the responsibility on your mate, it will be the number one reason you will soon find yourself lonely—again.

The Roots of the Reaction

When we dug deeper, Katie began to connect the dots. Her parents' addiction and abandonment had shaped how she viewed the world. The instability, moving from house to house, and never being truly wanted—those experiences taught her to expect rejection, to believe she wasn't valued. Her wild brain recorded these experiences as evidence and shaped her adult interactions based on them. It didn't care that her husband wasn't actually a threat. It didn't care about the context or the facts. It was operating from the only story it knew: **"You're not safe. Protect yourself."**

This narrative had caused her to perceive every neutral interaction—every innocent group message, every casual comment—as proof that her worst fears were about to come true.

Her wild brain believed that if she didn't react, she'd end up abandoned and alone again. And once her wild brain took the wheel, her observer brain went offline. The calm, rational part of her couldn't step in and say, "This is just a text. It's not an attack. He's not going anywhere." That part of her brain was silenced.

Breaking the Cycle

In our work together, I helped Katie start identifying what was stored in her wild brain. We dug into the specific experiences she'd been through, the thoughts she'd constructed about herself, and the intense feelings that bubbled up whenever those triggers were hit.

She began to see that her reactions were less about her husband's actions and more about her childhood baggage. She was finally able to identify her sh!t and own it.

"Wait, so every time I feel insecure, it's more than likely my wild brain is taking over?" she asked.

"Exactly," I said. "And when that happens, your observer brain—the part that can tell you what's really going on—gets shoved aside."

Katie and I began using the **Feelings Cycle** to break it down step-by-step. She started by listing her core feelings whenever she got triggered by something small—like that text message.

- **Feeling:** Unsafe and rejected

- **Thoughts:** "He's going to leave me. I'm not important to him"
- **Actions:** Yelling, accusing, pulling away emotionally

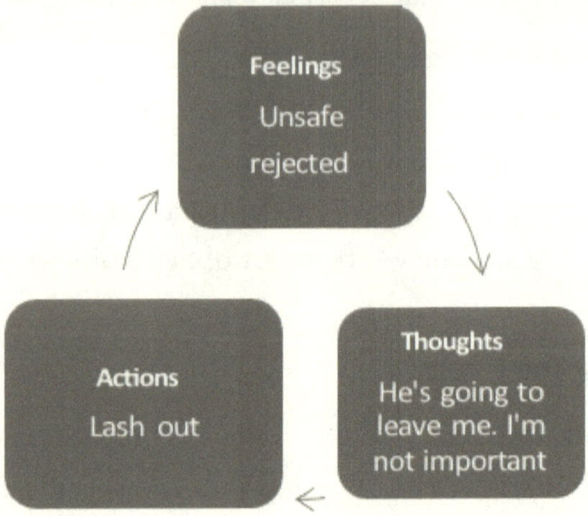

Feelings Cycle

Seeing it on paper was powerful for her. It was like holding a mirror up to her reactions, allowing her to see how her wild brain was spinning these thoughts and pushing her into destructive behaviors. And then, we shifted to the **Power Cycle**, where Katie started identifying the irrefutable truths that the wild brain conveniently ignored.

- **What I Know:** "I'm not alone. My husband is here because he loves me.
- **Irrefutable Truth:** I am loved by many people who have never rejected me, including my husband.

- **New Action:** "I will pause, breathe, and ask for support when I feel insecure or threatened instead of lashing out."

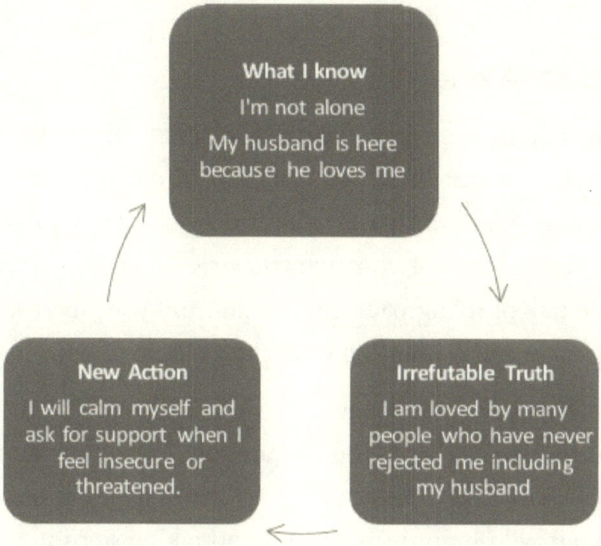

Power Cycle

Finding Her Observer Brain

By learning to step back and access her observer brain, Katie started to see her husband as he really was—not through the distorted lens of her wild brain. She started to understand that he wasn't the enemy, and her emotions weren't always reliable indicators of reality.

Katie began to communicate with her husband openly. Instead of accusing him, she expressed her feelings: "When I see group texts that include women, I experience feeling unwanted and rejected and it triggers feelings of insecurity in me because of my past. Can we talk about it?"

Her husband, no longer under attack and no longer feeling responsible for fixing her insecurity, was more than willing to support her. They started rebuilding trust, brick by brick.

You're Not Alone

Katie isn't an isolated case. Many of us unknowingly let our wild brains sabotage our lives. We react out of old wounds, stuck in survival mode, rather than responding from a place of awareness and strength. Some of you right now are charging someone else with the task of fixing your insecurities, and your mate is secretly pulling away and crumbling under the weight of your baggage.

But here's the good news: Katie is still married today. She learned to own her sh!t, and so can you. You're not doomed to repeat the same destructive patterns. The first step is recognizing when your wild brain is in control and taking steps to re-engage your observer brain. Katie was able to do the work, and I'm fully convinced you can too.

Remember, the wild brain thinks it knows everything because it's holding onto all those painful memories as evidence. But just because it's loud doesn't mean it's right.

If you see yourself in Katie's story—even just a little—it's time to take a hard look at the baggage you're carrying. What unhealed wounds are driving your reactions? What narratives are you clinging to that no longer serve you?

You don't have to let your wild brain run the show. By becoming aware of your patterns and doing the work to heal, you can break free from survival mode and start living—really living.

Let's go deeper.

QUESTION

When you feel insecure or threatened in your relationships, what old stories or beliefs might be fueling your reaction?

4

You're not broken—you're rehearsing old battles in new relationships. And calling it strength.

-Dr. Renee

"If you don't watch yourself, you're going to inadvertently become the father you despise."

Chapter Four

The Fighter

Dave stormed into my office visibly upset. The moment his wife started explaining how his outbursts terrified her, he snapped, "Well, apparently I'm doing everything wrong, so no sense in telling my side." His arms were folded tightly, his words laced with venom.

"Dave," I said softly, "if you don't watch yourself, you're going to inadvertently become the father you despise."

It was clear: Dave's wild brain was driving his life straight off a cliff.

But it didn't start here.

Dave's Story: Defensive Instincts

Dave was the eldest of eight siblings, forced to bear the brunt of an abusive father's rage while his mother passively stood by. He would often ask himself, "**What did I do to deserve this**?" Small and powerless, Dave couldn't fight back, so he learned to retreat to his room, feeling defeated and isolated. Over the years, the rage and resentment grew deep inside him like a cancer, until he made a vow to himself: **Never again**. No one would make him feel weak or powerless ever again.

So, when he felt threatened, he fought. He lashed out. He became defiant, determined to prove that he would never be a punching bag for anyone—at home, at work, or anywhere else. The problem was that this anger, this need to fight back, was fueled by unprocessed wild brain narratives from decades earlier. He wasn't defending himself from his wife, he was defending himself from his father. And he didn't even know it.

The Incident that Broke it Open

Dave's wife recounted a recent argument that perfectly encapsulated his wild brain at work. He had taken on the task of repainting their bedroom, determined, as always, to do a perfect job. He was almost finished when his wife casually mentioned, "I should've gone with a darker color." Dave immediately dropped the paintbrush, stormed out to the garage to watch TV, and later slept on the couch, avoiding any interaction with his wife. The next day, when his wife gently asked what was wrong, Dave exploded:

"It's clear **you don't appreciate me as your husband**. **I can't do anything right. I can never please you or anybody."**

What's really going on here?

His wild brain, always on standby, misinterpreted his wife's offhand comment as a direct attack—just like his father's verbal abuse. To his wild brain, her words weren't just a casual observation; they were a knife, stabbing into his core wound: **You're not good enough**.

When triggered, Dave didn't stop to think or reflect. His emotional brain took over, leaving his observer brain in the dust. He had only two options: shut down and retreat or stand up and fight. This same reaction was driven by deep-seated **feelings of inadequacy** and the haunting thought that he was always doing something wrong, that **he was never enough**.

This destructive cycle followed Dave to work, too, where any form of feedback or criticism sent him spiraling. Even a minor critique from a colleague would confirm his fear of inadequacy, pushing him to either shut down or become combative, making every job a battlefield.

The Bigger Picture

A lot of people think they know why relationships are failing today—but most of what they believe isn't true. We've latched onto empty, repetitive rhetoric spewed across social media, and it's spreading like a virus. Not only is it meaningless, it's toxic. And now, instead of showing up with curiosity or emotional maturity, people are approaching relationships like threats—using survival strategies to avoid being with a man who's not "high value" or a woman who isn't "feminine enough."

This kind of thinking has hijacked how we connect. The natural, human process of bonding—building trust, creating safety, extending grace—is being replaced by suspicion, rigidity, and performance. Nobody feels safe to be vulnerable. Trust is nonexistent. And before we've even taken the time to learn someone's story, we've already written them off based on superficial, unrealistic, and often made-up standards.

Let's be clear: This isn't about masculinity or femininity. It's not about being "high value." That's all noise.

The real problem is simpler and far more destructive: We're trying to build adult relationships using survival strategies we learned as scared little kids. Most people are still operating through the lens of childhood wounds. They're judging others through warped filters—shaped by trauma, neglect, abandonment, and fear—and calling it discernment. But what's really happening is that the child who had to hustle to feel safe is still running the show.

Dave's case is a great example of how whatever you had to become to survive as a kid devastates your adult life, without us even knowing it. **We sometimes become the monster because we had to survive one.**

Dave, like Katie, exemplifies how quickly we can slip into our emotional brains, letting our ability to think clearly and analyze situations accurately get hijacked. When this happens, we might as well be children again—reacting purely out of fear and confusion, trapped in survival mode because we're stuck in our wild and newborn brains.

Breaking the Cycle

Much of my work with Dave was helping him recognize when he was trapped in his emotional brain. We utilized the Feelings Cycle to expand his emotional vocabulary beyond the usual mad, sad, or angry. These are often the only feelings many people can identify because they were never taught to label their emotions beyond the basics.

Eventually, Dave was able to pinpoint that he wasn't just "angry" at his wife; he felt **deeply disappointed in himself**. This realization led him to connect his current feelings with those childhood moments when he felt like he had disappointed his father. From there, he identified the persistent thought that haunted him: **I'm not good enough**. And he finally saw his automatic reaction for what it was—an attempt to protect himself, whether that meant shutting down or lashing out.

By understanding and owning these ingrained responses, clients like Dave can start to shift from knee-jerk reactions to more thoughtful interactions, both in their personal lives and in their workplaces.

Creating Dave's Feelings Cycle

We mapped out Dave's feelings, thoughts, and actions in a cycle so he could see his pattern more clearly.

- **Feelings:** Disappointment and inadequacy
- **Thoughts:** "I'm not good enough. I can't do anything right"
- **Actions:** Lashing out, shutting down, and retreating emotionally

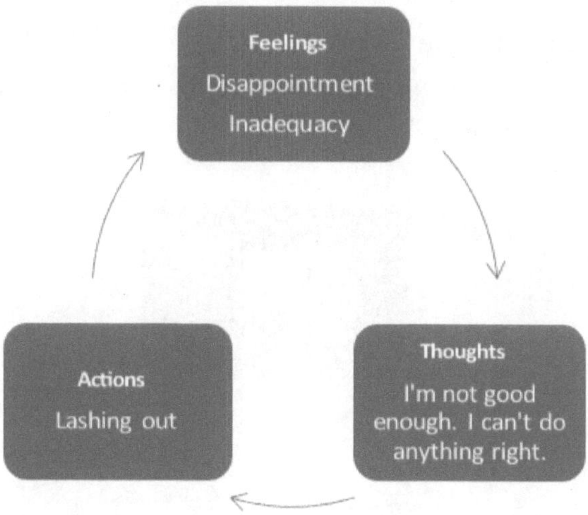

Feelings Cycle

Seeing this pattern in front of him helped Dave recognize how his wild brain had been running the show, reacting from old pain and outdated beliefs, not from the reality of his life today.

The Power Cycle: Changing the Narrative

Once we created his Feelings Cycle, we shifted to the **Power Cycle**, which helps clients identify what they **know** to be true instead of what they **feel** in the heat of the moment. This shift allows us to move from the wild brain to the observer (adult brain), and thus out of our emotional/survival brain.

- **What I Know:** "My wife has shown me patience and understanding."
- **Irrefutable Truth:** "I'm capable of being a loving, thoughtful husband."
- **New Action:** "When I feel triggered, I will take a moment to breathe and remind myself that this is about my past, not my wife."

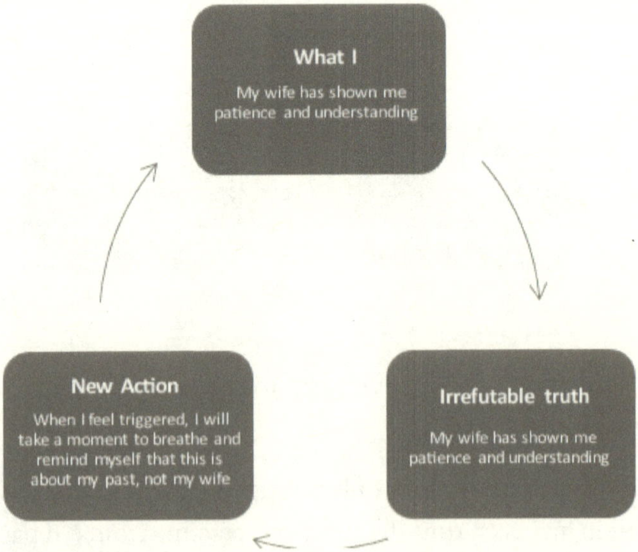

Power Cycle

Putting the Brakes on the Wild Brain

Each time Dave felt triggered, we practiced using the OWN Method:

1. **Observe What's happening Now:** Notice the immediate physical sensations: tightness in the chest, racing thoughts, tension in the shoulders. Become aware of the moment before you react.
2. **What part of my brain is running the show?:** Is this my wild brain reacting from old pain or my observer brain seeing things clearly?
3. **Name it:** "I'm feeling disappointed because I think I'm not good enough." This simple act of naming the feeling brought his observer brain back online, allowing him to take a pause.

Moving Beyond the Pain

Once Dave started using the Feelings Cycle and the Power Cycle, he noticed a shift. He was able to slow down his reactions, challenge his wild brain's narratives, and start responding differently. His wife, who had been bracing for his outbursts, was now seeing a calmer, more reflective version of Dave.

Breaking free from the grip of the wild brain isn't easy. It takes practice and patience. But it is possible. Dave's journey wasn't about becoming someone else; it was about reclaiming the part of him that could see the truth clearly—the part that knew he was enough, even when his wild brain said otherwise.

The OWN Method isn't an instant fix, and it's crucial to understand that real change takes time and consistent effort. However, while the results may not be immediate, the mindset shift that comes from recognizing and owning your baggage can happen instantly. When you begin to observe what's happening in the moment—when you catch yourself in an emotional reaction or triggered state—you start the process of regaining control over your responses. This awareness alone is powerful. It breaks the automatic cycle and allows you to pause and reflect. But the key to lasting change is to practice the OWN Method over time.

When you repeatedly engage your observer brain, you're training your brain to shift away from the automatic, knee-jerk reactions of the wild brain. Over time, this creates new pathways, strengthening your ability to respond with intentionality rather than out of raw emotion or survival instinct.

Initially, your wild brain will likely dominate in moments of stress, pulling you back into old patterns. But with each use of the OWN Method, you're rewiring your brain. You're teaching it to calm the automatic impulses that have governed your behavior for so long. Studies in neuroplasticity have demonstrated that when self-regulation practices—like mindfulness or intentional reflection—are done consistently, they create lasting changes in the brain. These changes are especially seen in the prefrontal cortex, the area of the brain associated with decision-making, problem-solving, and emotional regulation (observer brain).

What this means is that, with time, the OWN Method enables you to move from automatic, emotional reactions to well-thought-out, logical responses. You begin to rely less on the wild brain and more on the observer brain. Your responses become more reasonable, grounded in reality rather than in old narratives or emotional baggage.

The beauty of the OWN Method is that it provides a clear framework for how to break free from destructive cycles. But it requires dedication and practice. The more you apply it, the more your brain will adapt, allowing you to choose behaviors that align with who you truly are, rather than the automatic responses that were designed for survival but are no longer serving you.

In essence, the OWN Method doesn't promise a quick fix, but it does offer the potential for deep, transformative change. By committing to this practice over time, you're not just changing how you think or feel in the moment—you're literally reshaping how your brain functions. With that, you gain the power to shift from being reactive to intentional, which ultimately leads to healthier relationships, more grounded decision-making, and a greater sense of control over your life.

We're just scratching the surface here. If you see bits of Dave or any of the other clients in your reactions or interactions, it's time to delve deeper and really own your emotional responses. Let's move beyond surviving on old, unhelpful instincts and start thriving with conscious, thoughtful behaviors.

QUESTION

What automatic reactions or defense mechanisms do you rely on when you feel criticized or threatened, and how might they be affecting your relationships?

5

“As long as you stay committed to their wrongs, you’ll stay blind to your wounds.”

-Dr. Renee

"You two are baking a crazy cake, and both of you are showing up with ingredients."

Chapter Five

The Blame Game

Greg and Stephanie sat across from me, their body language speaking louder than words—both carrying the weight of disappointment and frustration. Greg's arms were tightly crossed, his jaw clenched, and his stare intense enough to burn holes through the walls. Stephanie mirrored his posture, eyes sharp, her voice dripping with bitterness.

"I just don't trust him anymore," she said, emphasizing each word like a blade slicing through the air. "He let me down in a major way."

Each sentence seemed to tighten Greg's expression, drawing his shoulders higher and higher, his frustration building until he finally erupted. "She acts like I killed someone!" he spat, his voice heavy with hurt. **"I made one mistake, and she'll never let it go. I'm done."**

This wasn't just a marital spat. This was a full-scale emotional war fueled by deep, unhealed wounds from their pasts, both of them stuck in a never-ending loop of accusation and defensiveness, unable to access the part of their brains that could help them see the truth—the Observer Brain. Instead, they were trapped in the Wild Brain, reacting from a place of pain and fear rather than logic and love. I knew it was vital to show them that they both were contributing to the conflict. "You two are baking a crazy cake, and both of you are showing up with ingredients," I said, "You can stop blaming the other person, both of you are contributing equally." It was important they understood that both of them were bringing ingredients of unresolved pain and blame from their past—creating something volatile.

It's Never Just One Person

In sessions like this, I often hear clients say, "If he would just stop doing X," or, "If she didn't always do Y, we wouldn't have these problems." It's easy to blame the other person when we're hurting, to point fingers and assign blame, thinking it's just one person causing all the chaos. But I've found that in most cases, it's never just one person. It's a cycle—a tangled mess of feelings, thoughts, and automatic actions that lock the two people in a destructive pattern.

My study of couples has confirmed this. When couples come in, they're convinced it's their partner's fault. He did this; she did that. But what I see are two **Wild Brains** caught in a vicious cycle, each person's pain triggering the other's. And here's the most important part: When both partners can step back and identify their own baggage, regulate it, and engage their Observer Brain, the conflict and arguments tend to de-escalate. The severity of the difficulties diminishes.

It's like a dance, but not the romantic kind. It's a painful waltz of hurt and reaction, each person stepping on the other's toes over and over again. The key is to stop blaming the other person and start owning your own sh!t—because as long as you're stuck pointing fingers, you're trapped in the cycle.

Stephanie's Story: Understanding the Emotional Hijack

Let's look at Stephanie. She was an only child, growing up in a home where her parents set impossible standards and constantly reminded her how she always fell short. She spent her formative years being belittled, criticized, and emotionally neglected. Every disappointment was a confirmation that she wasn't good enough. Eventually, she began to rebel, acting out and getting into trouble at school. By the time she was seventeen, her anger and resentment got her into serious trouble, leading to a brief stint in a juvenile detention facility.

When she called her parents, begging for help, they turned their backs on her. Instead of welcoming her home, they made it clear she was no longer welcome under their roof. She was shipped off to her grandmother's house, her only safe haven. Worse still, she discovered that her parents had shared every mistake and every failure with the entire family, broadcasting her pain for all to see. From that moment on, she vowed never to trust anyone again. Her grandmother was the only person who stood by her.

To survive, Stephanie built walls so high no one could penetrate them. She couldn't bear the thought of being exposed and humiliated again, so she fought tooth and nail to protect herself, attacking anyone who made her feel vulnerable. If there was even a hint of betrayal, she would strike first to avoid being wounded.

Greg's Story: A Childhood Shaped by One Mistake

Then there was Greg. His childhood was marred by a single, catastrophic mistake that haunted him well into adulthood. At eight years old, his curiosity got the best of him, and he set a small fire in his bedroom that quickly spiraled out of control. His grandmother was inside the house at the time and barely escaped. In the days that followed, the family erupted in chaos, screaming at Greg about how he had almost killed his grandmother, how he could have burned down the entire house.

From then on, every family gathering was a reminder of his failure. They wouldn't let him forget it. It became the story told at every holiday—"Remember when Greg almost burned down the house?"— an anecdote shared with a mix of humor and resentment that twisted the knife deeper each time. By the time Greg reached adulthood, the narrative was set: **He was dangerous. His mistakes were deadly**. And he believed it. To protect himself, he avoided confrontation at all costs, doing everything he could to be "perfect" so no one could hold his mistakes against him.

The Incident That Triggered the Crisis

Fast forward to today. Greg and Stephanie's marriage, which had started strong, was unraveling fast. The breaking point came when Stephanie's grandmother fell gravely ill. She asked Greg to come with her to visit, desperate for his support. But he couldn't leave work, so she went alone—emotionally flooded, unsupported, and silently managing her own grief and fear. Then she saw it—a post on social media showing Greg with his friends at a bar the same day he was "too busy" to be with her. That image shattered what little trust she had left. To Stephanie's Wild Brain, this wasn't just a slight; **it was betrayal**. A confirmation that she couldn't count on him, just like she couldn't count on her parents. Her worst fears—abandonment, rejection, humiliation—were all coming true.

When she got home, she lashed out. The argument escalated, spiraled, and finally exploded. Greg, caught off guard, was immediately on the defensive. His Wild Brain leapt into action, convinced he was being unfairly attacked for something he couldn't control. His internal narrative was on repeat: **You're a screw-up. Your mistakes are unforgivable**. After several heated arguments, Greg shut down, only making Stephanie feel more rejected.

The Wild Brain Takes Over

It got so bad that the police were called. Stephanie, who had been the aggressor, was asked to leave the house temporarily because her behavior was deemed threatening. She had screamed at Greg, gotten in his face, and even made motions to strike him.

Greg, meanwhile, was trapped in his own Wild Brain narrative. He couldn't see that Stephanie's rage was fueled by a lifetime of rejection and betrayal. All he saw was that he had made one tiny mistake, and once again, the consequences were catastrophic. His body language screamed one message: **You'll never forgive me, no matter what I do**.

In our sessions, I taught Greg and Stephanie how to identify their feelings, thoughts, and actions. We then created their combined feelings cycle so they had a visual of how their thoughts and actions kept them locked up in a destructive cycle. It doesn't matter if we start with Stephanie's or Greg's Feelings, it's their automatic behaviors that perpetuate the cycle. For instance, when Stephanie starts to feel rejected, she lashes out. Greg, in turn, feels humiliated and starts to shut down or lash out, only causing Stephanie to feel rejected again.

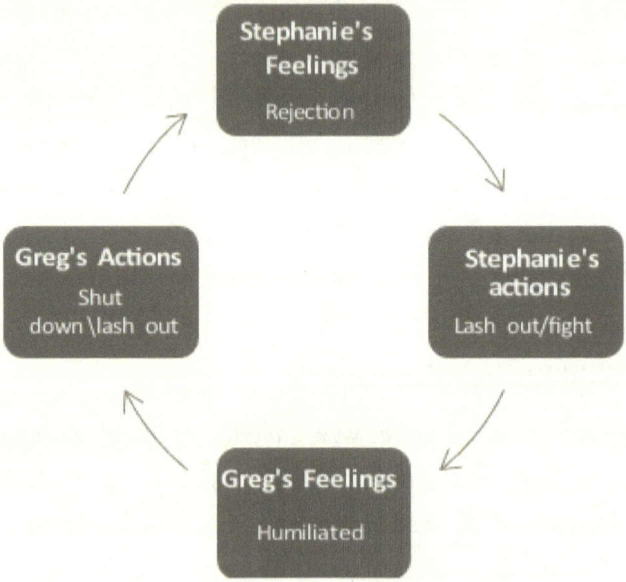

Their conflicts were a clear demonstration of being stuck in the Wild and Newborn Brain states, where rational thought is offline and they were unable to access the Observer Brain, which could provide a more accurate interpretation of the events.

Breaking the Cycle

Greg identified **humiliation**, linking it back to the childhood incident that continued to define him. Stephanie recognized her feelings of **rejection**, rooted in her lifelong sense of inadequacy instilled by her parents.

They learned to utilize the three critical questions during heated moments:

1. **What do I feel?**
2. **What are my thoughts?**
3. **What are my typical actions or reactions?**

The three questions helped them step back from the brink, allowing their Observer Brains to come online and reassess the situation with clarity.

They began to see not just their own behaviors but each other's perspectives more clearly. Greg realized that Stephanie's reaction was about seeking support, not attacking him. Stephanie saw that Greg's mistake was not a betrayal but an unfortunate oversight.

Moving Forward

This is the crux of real change—recognizing and owning our emotional responses, becoming aware of our Wild Brain's narratives, and choosing to engage our Observer Brain instead.

Let's go deeper.

QUESTION

In moments of conflict, how often do you rely on blaming others instead of examining your own emotional triggers?

6

"If you don't learn to tell the difference between danger and discomfort, ***you'll keep quitting peace to protect your pain."***

-Dr. Renee

“I’ve been running away from sticks my whole life.”

Chapter Six

It's a Snake!

When Brandy walked into my office, her anxiety was palpable. She perched on the edge of the couch, clutching her notepad like a lifeline. Brandy was the type of client that had been running from ghosts of the past for many years without even knowing. This was our fourth session, and I could see that something had clicked. She barely let me settle in before she blurted out, "I've realized something important."

Brandy was feeling overwhelmed with her current employment status. She was in between jobs, which was unsettling for her given she was highly skilled and held several degrees. While she was surprised to find herself unemployed—again, this wasn't the first time she had walked away from a corporate job. However, this was the first time she knew why.

"Oh yeah? What's that?" I asked, leaning forward.

She took a deep breath. "As I've been working on my feelings cycle, I've started remembering where my feelings really come from. **It's like I've been running from ghosts**."

Brandy's Story: Life is a Battlefield

Brandy was an only child whose childhood was dominated by trauma and fear. Her biological mother had passed away when she was just eight, leaving her alone with her father and his wife—a woman who made it clear that Brandy would never be welcome.

From that point on, Brandy was caught in a relentless cycle of verbal and physical abuse from her stepmother, while her father did nothing to intervene.

The household was a war zone. Brandy's days were filled with screams and insults, slaps and bruises, and a constant sense of fear. But what made it even worse was her father's silence. He would sit there, eyes averted, letting it all happen. No protection. No comfort. No love. The message was clear: Brandy didn't matter. She wasn't worth protecting.

To survive, she learned to stay alert, to be hyper-vigilant. She became a master at predicting when the next storm would hit, always on edge, always watching for the next explosion. She would spend hours hiding in her room, clutching her stuffed bear, straining to hear her stepmother's footsteps in the hall, wondering if this was going to be one of the "bad days."

As soon as she was old enough, Brandy escaped the toxic environment by getting her own place. The physical abuse stopped, but the verbal assaults continued every time she visited. Even after Brandy had her own child, her stepmother would launch into brutal tirades about her parenting, leaving Brandy feeling just as **small and powerless** as she did when she was eight years old.

"**I often feel threatened**," Brandy admitted. **"I'm constantly on guard, like I'm just waiting for the next attack."**

The Snake in the Park

Here's the thing: When we're overwhelmed by fear or stress, our Wild Brain sees danger where there isn't any. I explained this to Brandy by using an analogy I borrowed from Bessel van der Kolk, it's called "The Snake in the Park."

"Imagine you're taking a walk through a beautiful park," I began. "But then, out of the corner of your eye, you see it—a snake! Instantly, your body goes into overdrive. Your heart races, your muscles tighten, and you leap back, desperate to get away. Then, after catching your breath and calming down, you take a closer look, only to find that it's not a snake at all—it's a stick."

This is your survival brain—the Newborn Brain—at work. When faced with what appears to be a threat, the Newborn Brain springs into action to protect you. It's automatic and instantaneous. Before your Observer Brain—the rational part of your mind—can analyze what's really happening, you're already reacting. Your Wild Brain, which stores old pain and fears, lights up, screaming, **"You're in danger! Run! Fight! Escape!"**

Your Wild Brain doesn't pause to find out if it's a snake, it just reacts from the wild story of **"You're in danger!"** It hijacks you into fight-or-flight mode because it believes the threat is real. And by the time your Observer Brain catches up, you've already taken action based on that fear—jumped back, screamed, or even ran away.

That's what was happening to Brandy every time she felt criticized at work. Her Wild Brain was convinced she was in danger, reacting as if she were that small, powerless child again.

The Wild Brain's Automatic Reaction

Brandy's Wild Brain was holding on to old childhood narratives: **I'm not safe. Someone's going to hurt me. I'm always going to be attacked.** Her body reacted accordingly, tensing up, bracing for impact, even when there was no real threat in front of her. She would get nervous at work, tense up at home, and feel panicked in new situations. Her entire life was ruled by a phantom snake that didn't exist.

When Brandy started a new job, she was always well-prepared and skilled enough to meet high-level expectations. Her supervisors praised her intelligence and work ethic. But inevitably, someone would offer a minor critique—a small comment about her presentation style, or a suggestion to refine her approach. To Brandy's Wild Brain, that minor feedback was a snake.

Before her Observer Brain could step in and analyze the situation, her Newborn Brain went straight into survival mode: **Fight or flight! Protect yourself! Get out before it gets worse!** She interpreted the critique as proof that she was **failing, that she wasn't good enough, that she was about to be exposed as an imposter.** Then, her reaction was automatic—shut down, become defensive, or quit the job entirely.

Brandy's Wild Brain reacted out of fear, convincing her that if she didn't get out, she would be destroyed. So, she would plan her escape and leave, quitting before she had a chance to see that she was, in fact, doing great work.

It wasn't until after she left that Brandy would look back and realize, ***I was thriving. I was actually skilled enough. I was being noticed, not criticized.*** But by then, it was too late. She had already taken the drastic action of quitting, and the cycle would start all over again.

The Maladaptive Cycle

Here's what Brandy's destructive cycle looked like:

1. **Trigger:** A small critique or suggestion.
2. **Feeling:** Fear and anxiety, rooted in childhood abuse and neglect.
3. **Thoughts:** I'm not good enough. I'm going to fail. I'm going to be humiliated again.
4. **Action:** Shut down, run away, quit the job.

This same cycle played out in every corporate role Brandy took on. Despite her qualifications, skills, and intelligence, she kept ending up in the same place: unemployed and back to square one, searching for a new position, terrified of repeating the pattern but inevitably falling into it again.

Brandy's Wild Brain was running her life, and the only way to break free was to bring her Observer Brain back online.

Getting the Observer Brain Back Online

When your Wild Brain is triggered, it hijacks your entire system. Your Newborn Brain springs into action, reacting out of pure instinct, and your Observer Brain goes offline. When you're in survival mode, you're not thinking rationally. You're not seeing the facts. You're reacting from old stories and pain, convinced that the situation is dangerous, even if it's not.

Brandy's challenge was to slow down, let her Observer Brain catch up, and give herself time to see the situation clearly. That's where the **Feelings Cycle** came in. We started breaking down her patterns using the three critical questions:

1. **What do I feel?**
2. **What are my thoughts?**

3. **What are my typical actions or reactions?**

For Brandy, the answer was clear. When she felt **threatened** (feeling), her thoughts immediately went to, ***I'm going to mess up. I'm not good enough. I'm going to get hurt.*** And her reaction? To shut down and quit.

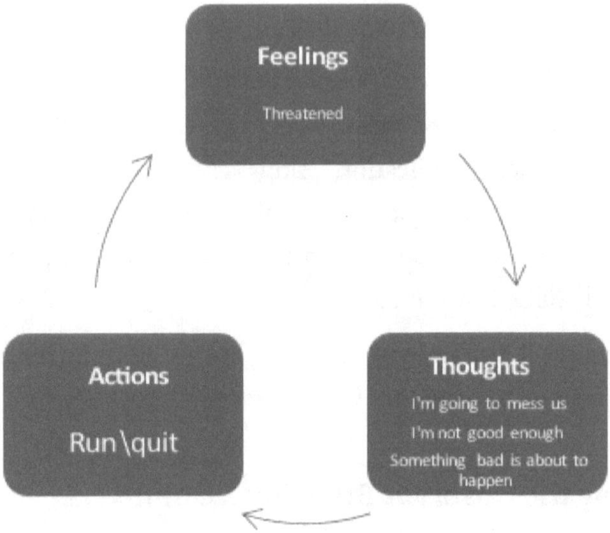

Feelings Cycle

"This cycle has been running your life," I said. "And the only way to break it is to identify it, own it, and bring your Observer Brain back into the driver's seat."

Breaking Free from Phantom Snakes

Brandy's journey wasn't easy, but with time and practice, she learned to pause before reacting. When she felt the familiar wave of anxiety rising, she would stop and ask herself: **Is this really a snake?** Most of the time, the answer was no. It was just a stick.

Her Wild Brain had been seeing threats everywhere, convincing her that every small critique or minor conflict was a snake ready to strike. But now she was starting to see the truth. Most of those threats weren't real.

"I've been running for no reason," she whispered, shaking her head. ***"I've been running away from sticks my whole life."***

Moving Forward

Brandy's story isn't unique. So many people run from phantom snakes—imaginary threats created by the Wild Brain, driven by old narratives that no longer serve them. The key is to slow down, let the Observer Brain catch up, and see the situation clearly before reacting. Because when we don't, we keep repeating the same destructive cycles.

But if we can pause, breathe, and see things for what they are, we might just find that the things we've been running from were never snakes at all.

QUESTION

What sticks in your life have you mistaken for snakes?

7

"You learned to equate silence with strength. *But your real power is in the truth you're scared to say out loud."*

-Dr. Renee

These lies keep us trapped, sacrificing, and locked in toxic situations. But the truth—the irrefutable truth—is that we are worthy. We are good enough. We've already proven it.

Chapter Seven

Lie Vs the Irrefutable Truth

Emulu first walked into my office like a man who'd just crawled out of a burning house—smoke still clinging to him, soul scorched, eyes hollow from years of pretending he wasn't on fire. His wife had already abandoned therapy, unwilling to confront her own demons, leaving him to unravel their crumbling marriage alone. This man had spent years sacrificing himself to make his wife happy, only to be met with betrayal after betrayal. She'd cheated, lied, and emotionally abandoned him, but still, he stayed—each time convincing himself that if he just tried a little harder, he could fix things. Every week, he came in more defeated than the last, his spirit slowly eroding under the constant rejection.

Eventually, it broke him. He spiraled into a deep depression, drowning in thoughts of suicide, until one day, he was admitted to a facility for evaluation. It was during his stay there that he finally allowed himself to confront the depth of his pain. He was finally ready to be honest with himself about how many times he had caught his wife cheating, and how, each time, he'd chosen forgiveness over confrontation. But this wasn't forgiveness out of love—it was forgiveness driven by desperation, by a deep-seated fear that if he didn't, he would lose everything. Because underneath it all was a lie he had been telling himself his entire life: **I'm not a good husband. I'm a bad father. I'm unworthy of love, and if I don't keep trying, I'll be abandoned.**

Emulu's Story: The Origin of the Lie

Emulu's story started far from the office we sat in. He was born and raised in a small village in Africa—where his feelings of inadequacy first took root. When he was just five years old, his mother left him. She walked out and never looked back, leaving Emulu to fend for himself with an emotionally unavailable father who was more prone to rage than to love. His father eventually remarried, but his stepmother was no savior. The house turned into a battlefield, with daily screaming matches, insults hurled like grenades, and physical fights breaking out at the slightest provocation. Although his father hadn't left as his mom had, Emulu felt equally abandoned and rejected by his father.

Caught in the middle, little Emulu learned to stay quiet, to make himself invisible. Any time he dared speak up, he was met with, "Why can't you just be quiet?" or "You're the problem in this house!" So, he stayed silent, **becoming a shadow in his own home**.

His voice—his needs, his pain—didn't matter. The adults fought over him, around him, and sometimes with him, but never for him. He learned that the best way to survive was to **become invisible**. If he could just be a good, quiet boy, maybe they would stop yelling. Maybe he wouldn't be hurt.

His only refuge was his grandmother—a gentle, loving woman who showed him the care and acceptance he'd never received from his parents. With her, he felt safe. But just when he thought he'd finally found a place where he belonged, she passed away, leaving him alone again. The message was clear: **Everyone I love will leave me. I'll never be good enough for them to stay.**

The Trap of Survival Mode

Desperate to escape the pain and emptiness of his childhood, Emulu left for the United States at eighteen. Here, he met a woman who seemed to offer everything he'd ever wanted—a sense of family and belonging. Her family welcomed him with open arms, and for the first time, he felt he was part of something stable and good. But his relationship with her was flawed from the start. She was unfaithful even before they were married. When she became pregnant, Emulu wasn't even sure the child was his. Despite the warning signs, he married her anyway. Why? **Because he was terrified of being alone. Terrified of being abandoned again.**

The lie whispered in his ear: **If you were a better man, she'd stay. If you leave, it proves you're a failure.**

For years, he endured her infidelity in silence. Every time he caught her cheating, every time she was unfaithful, that lie would rear its ugly head: **This is your fault. If you were better, if you were stronger, if you were worthy, she wouldn't be doing this.** Confrontation wasn't an option. Confrontation meant conflict, and conflict meant rejection. Rejection meant being alone. And that was a fate Emulu couldn't bear to face.

Instead, he doubled down on his efforts to make her happy. He cut ties with friends and family, isolating himself to focus solely on his wife and children. He bent over backward to cater to her every whim, hoping against hope that one day she'd see his worth. But no matter what he did, it was never enough. She continued her affairs, continued to disrespect him, continued to treat him like an afterthought. And Emulu stayed, a prisoner to the lie that had been planted in his childhood: **I'm a bad husband and father. I'm not good enough. If I leave, I'll be proving that I'm a failure.**

Paralyzed By the Lies

What Emulu didn't see was that he was living in survival mode every day. Just like the snake analogy in the previous chapter, he wasn't able to see the situation clearly because his Wild Brain was reacting to the lie embedded deep within him. He may not have thought it was a literal snake, but his reactions were based on a fear that wasn't grounded in reality. **If I leave, I'm just like my father.** This fear paralyzed him, keeping him locked in a marriage that was draining the life out of him.

When we are in survival mode, our Wild Brain hijacks our rational thinking, locking the Observer Brain out. Emulu's Observer Brain couldn't tell him the irrefutable truths about himself—that he had, in fact, done everything his parents hadn't. He hadn't abandoned his children. He had been present. He had been loyal. But none of this registered because the Wild Brain kept screaming: **If you leave, you're abandoning your family, just like your mother abandoned you.**

The Breakthrough

It wasn't until Emulu moved out of the house that he finally began to see the truth. The physical separation allowed his survival brain to calm down, and for the first time in years, he was able to access his Observer Brain. He began to see the irrefutable truths about himself and the situation.

He saw that he wasn't his father. He hadn't abandoned his children.

He hadn't left out of selfishness. He had stayed, supported, and provided for his family, even when his wife gave him every reason to walk away.

He saw that his wife's behavior wasn't his fault. Her infidelity wasn't a reflection of his worth—it was a reflection of her own choices and issues.

And most importantly, he realized that leaving didn't make him a failure. It made him a man who valued himself enough to walk away from someone who didn't. He wasn't abandoning his family; he was saving himself.

Breaking the Cycle

As Emulu discovered the irrefutable truth about himself and the situation, he started to set himself free. He finally left his wife and was living on his own for the first time in years. He had made several attempts to move out in the past, only to return weeks later, but this time he was determined not to return. He looked lighter, freer. There was a quiet strength in his eyes that hadn't been there before.

"I don't have to stay," he said quietly, as if testing the words. "I can leave and still be a good father. I can leave and still be a good man."

"Yes, I agree," I said. "It's been clear to me the entire time that you were a great father and exceptional husband, I was just waiting for you to discover that for yourself."

Embracing the Irrefutable Truth

Emulu's journey is a powerful reminder of the lies we tell ourselves. These lies keep us trapped, sacrificing, and locked in toxic situations. But the truth—the irrefutable truth—is that we are worthy. We are good enough. We've already proven it. When we see that, we unlock the power to break free, to honor ourselves, and to build lives that reflect our true worth. It is imperative that you understand that anytime your wild brain is activated, it's going to hijack your ability to have access to your observer brain, which is where the irrefutable truths are located. I have watched clients stay in toxic situations far too long because they remained in the house, which meant every day, they were surviving, struggling with extreme emotions and reacting in ways that only confirmed their feeling of powerlessness. Your sh!t is powerful in that way; not only does it stink up your life but shuts down the most important part of your brain, leaving you only with wild thoughts and automatic behaviors—in essence, keeping you locked up with the lies.

Emulu's journey reminds us that the lies we believe about ourselves have deep roots, but they don't have to define us. By embracing irrefutable truths, we free ourselves to make choices that reflect our worth, not our fears.

QUESTION

What lie are you telling yourself that keeps you from living authentically? And what truths have you forgotten along the way?

8

"You're not fighting each other—you're fighting the pain you never named. *But until you own your wound, your partner will always look like the enemy."*

-Dr. Renee

It was deeply embedded in his mind, a shadow from his past, replaying the same painful script over and over.

Chapter Eight

The Dance of Destruction

"I'm tired of fighting," Sophie murmured, slumping in the chair like she was carrying a thousand pounds. Dewayne, her husband, sat across from her, his fists clenched, rage radiating off him in waves. He had been fired up from the moment he walked into my office, convinced that Sophie saw no value in him. He was ready to pounce, to explode, to force her to say something that would validate the fury boiling inside him.

"She's always telling me I ain't Shit," Dewayne spat, his voice trembling with anger. He had his list of grievances—every moment where he felt slighted, every instance where he thought Sophie wasn't in his corner, wasn't defending him. One incident in particular seemed to replay in his mind on an endless loop.

"I got into a fight with my cousin," he recalled, his voice rising. "My cousin was talking all this shit about me, calling me a loser, saying I'm worthless. And what did Sophie do? Nothing! She just sat there and didn't say a word. Then she just got up, walked out to the car, and left me there to fend for myself."

He turned his gaze back to Sophie, eyes blazing, waiting for an answer. He wanted her to explain, to justify her silence, to admit that she thought he was worthless, just like everyone else did.

But Sophie didn't lash back. She didn't defend herself. She just sighed—a deep, weary sound—and looked down at her lap. **"I'm tired of fighting**, Dewayne," she said quietly. "I've spent a lifetime fighting men in my life. I'm exhausted. I don't have it in me anymore."

Hearing Voices from the Past

Dewayne's anger faltered. He glanced away, his body deflating as he tried to process what she was saying.

"It doesn't matter how much I tell you I love you," Sophie continued, her voice soft but steady. "It's never enough."

She was right. Throughout our sessions, it became clear that Sophie had never said the words Dewayne heard in his head—"You ain't shit." But he was convinced she had. And in a way, she had—because that voice he kept hearing was real, but it wasn't Sophie's. It was deeply embedded in his mind, a shadow from his past, replaying the same painful script over and over.

Dewayne's Story: The Roots of the Pain

Dewayne grew up with three other brothers. While his siblings all had relationships with their fathers, Dewayne was the outcast. His father was long gone, refusing to have anything to do with him. His brothers would return from weekends spent with their dads, boasting about all the fun they had. They came back with new clothes, money for school trips, and stories of fathers who cared. Dewayne had nothing. His mother, a single parent struggling to make ends meet, took out her frustrations on him. When his father didn't show up, she looked at Dewayne like he was the problem. "**You ain't shit, just like your daddy**," she'd hiss, her face twisted with anger.

It was a dagger to a child's heart. Those words cut deep, taking root in his wild brain, etching themselves into his self-concept. His brothers echoed her sentiments, mocking him, reminding him at every opportunity that he was nothing. "**You're just like him—a piece of trash.**" He heard it so often that it became his truth. The lie his wild brain fed him every time someone didn't stand up for him, didn't choose him, didn't fight for him.

Sophie's Story: Battles and Withdrawals

Sophie's story wasn't much different. While she had both parents at home, the environment was a war zone. They fought violently—screaming, hitting, throwing things. And when they weren't tearing each other apart, her father's rage turned on her. He'd trap her in a corner, spitting venomous words in her face while her mother watched passively, saying nothing. Sophie learned to endure. She knew she'd get no protection from her mother. Only later, when her father's rage had burned itself out, would her mother come to her, quietly asking if she was okay.

But Sophie never was okay. Her mother's silence, her refusal to intervene, made Sophie **feel abandoned**. As she grew older, the abuse escalated. Her father would lash out, her mother would beg her to leave for her own safety but wouldn't lift a finger to protect her. Sophie finally left, but the hell didn't end. Moving from one relative's house to another, she found herself preyed upon by male relatives who saw her as an easy target. When she tried to speak up, the women in the family blamed her, accusing her of provoking the men with her clothes or her behavior.

"I was fifteen," she'd said during one of our sessions, her voice hollow. "I was a kid, but it didn't matter. I had to fight off men in the house, and if I tried to tell anyone, I'd get beaten for it. **I learned to keep quiet**. To avoid. To run."

The Destructive Cycle

As we dove deeper into their stories, it became clear that they were caught in a destructive cycle. Dewayne's rage and accusations were met with Sophie's withdrawal and avoidance, which only made things worse for both of them. When Dewayne responded by lashing out, Sophie felt more helpless and powerless. The more she withdrew, the more Dewayne felt abandoned and rejected. This cycle trapped them in an endless loop of pain, each reacting to the other's pain and only amplifying the hurt they both felt.

1. **Dewayne feels betrayed.** When Sophie doesn't speak up, his wild brain activates and tells him, "She doesn't care. You're worthless."
2. **He lashes out in rage.** He yells, accuses, and tries to force her to prove she loves him.
3. **Sophie feels terrified and powerless.** His rage reminds her of her father's abuse, triggering her flight response.
4. **She withdraws or runs.** She either physically leaves or emotionally shuts down, trying to protect herself.
5. **Dewayne feels abandoned and betrayed again.** Her withdrawal confirms his deepest fear—that he's not good enough, that no one values him.
6. **The cycle starts again.** Each time it repeats, the pain and distance between them grow.

Breaking the Cycle

The work with Dewayne and Sophie wasn't just about talking through their problems—it was about recognizing this pattern and dismantling it piece by piece. They needed to see that their reactions were feeding off each other. Each time one flinched, the other struck harder. It wasn't connection, it was survival mode, and they were stuck in a loop that was tearing them apart.

By using the Feelings Cycle, we were able to map out what they were truly experiencing in those moments and see the cycle clearly.

Dewayne's Feelings Cycle:

- **Feeling:** Betrayed
- **Thought:** "She doesn't care. I'm worthless"
- **Action:** Lash out in anger

Sophie's Feelings Cycle:

- **Feeling:** Powerless and terrified
- **Thought:** "I can't stop him. I'm not safe"
- **Action:** Withdraw and run

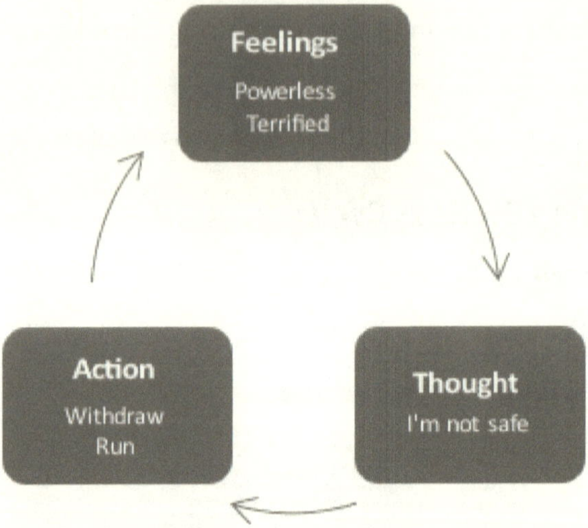

When they could see this pattern, they understood how their wild brains were hijacking their relationship. But understanding alone wasn't enough. They needed to break the cycle. Dewayne and Sophie needed a way to see past their own pain and fear—to create a moment's pause that could let them respond thoughtfully instead of just reacting.

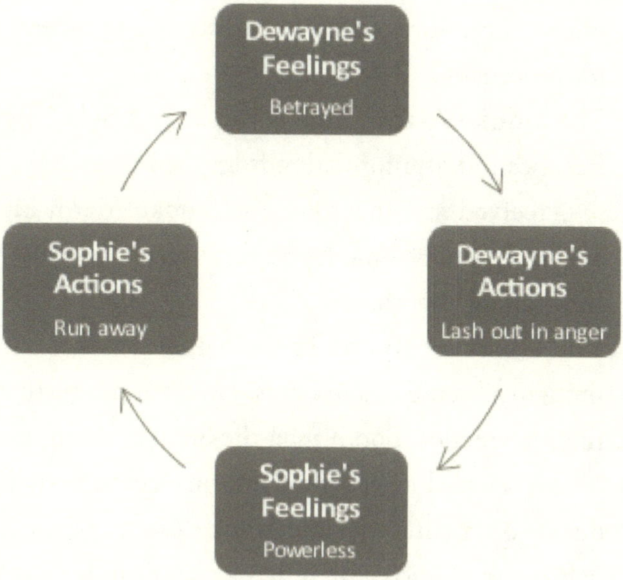

Combined Feelings Cycle

Shifting to the Power Cycle

In moments of dysregulation, if we can calm ourselves, we create enough space for our brains to observe the situation, identify feelings, and interpret the reality accurately.

Remember the "snake" scenario: Sometimes, we see something alarming, assign a fearful story to it, and react—all before calming down enough for our brain to catch up and correctly interpret the situation. This process unfolds because of how our brain is structured, and understanding this can be incredibly powerful.

Let's break it down simply. I use three nicknames to describe the parts of the brain at play here: the "Information Booth," the "Smoke Alarm," and the "Observer Brain."

1. **The Information Booth**: This part of the brain gathers information from our senses and sends it to different areas for processing.
2. **The Smoke Alarm**: This is the brain's fight, flight, or freeze center. If information from the Information Booth is perceived as dangerous, the Smoke Alarm kicks in, activating survival mode. It's fast because it's close to the Information Booth.
3. **The Observer Brain**: This is where we make logical, thoughtful sense of situations. However, it's further from the Information Booth than the Smoke Alarm, meaning it takes a little longer for the information to get here. This distance explains why the Smoke Alarm can sound off before the Observer Brain has a chance to intervene and set things straight.

When information first reaches the Smoke Alarm, we often react based on fear or past narratives—like Dewayne's feelings of betrayal or Sophie's feeling of powerlessness. This reaction is automatic, trapping them in a cycle where they're both "seeing the snake" over and over. To break this cycle, they need to bring truth into the moment.

The Power Cycle combats these wild narratives by grounding us in irrefutable truths—truths that are already proven and undeniable. These truths interrupt the Smoke Alarm's influence, giving the Observer Brain time to analyze.

In real-life situations, this is where the Power Cycle shines. For example, Dewayne was convinced he was being betrayed, and Sophie felt powerless. These feelings led directly to automatic reactions. But the Power Cycle helped by introducing three grounding questions that allowed the truth to slow things down, giving the Observer Brain a chance to take over:

1. **What do I know for sure?**
2. **What is the irrefutable truth about me?**
3. **What will I choose to do differently?**

For Dewayne, it looked like this:

- **What do I know for sure?** "My wife values my protection. She feels safe because of me."
- **What is the irrefutable truth?** "My wife has only proven how much she loves and respects me. I've been a loving, protective father and husband for many years."
- **What will I choose to do?** "I will not fight with her. I will calm down, knowing this little eight-year-old inside me is the one feeling betrayed, but that's not my reality."

For Sophie, it was:

- **What do I know for sure?** "Dewayne loves me and wants to protect me."
- **What is the irrefutable truth?** "I've learned to stand up for myself. I'm strong and capable."
- **What will I choose to do?** "I will not run. I will try to communicate my fear instead of shutting down."

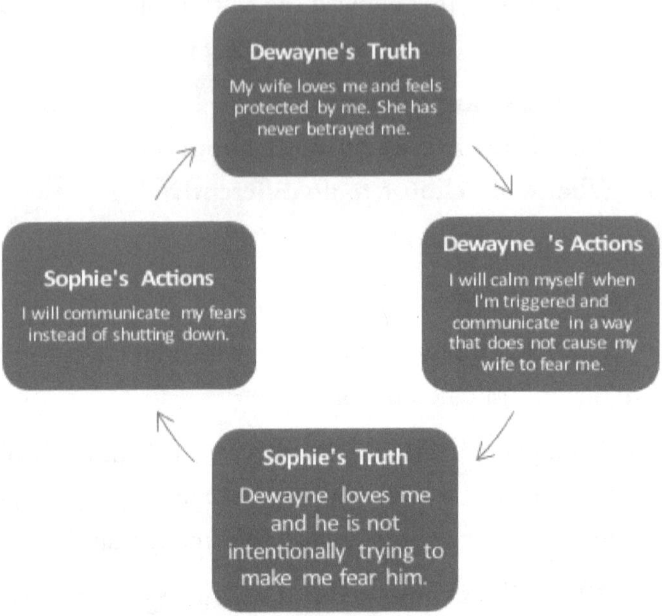

The Importance of Regulation

Through my work and study of couples, I found that when two people can regulate themselves and calm their emotional brains, their difficulties are significantly decreased. More importantly, when they feel equipped to handle their triggers, their sense of self-worth increases. It's not just about stopping the conflict—it's about empowering them to feel capable and in control of their emotions.

My study revealed that when arguments escalate, it's usually because neither person has the tools to regulate. They have no idea what to do but blame each other, perpetuating the cycle. But when both partners have the ability to recognize and own their emotional reactions, the willingness to regulate increases exponentially. They stop being two adversaries locked in battle and start becoming allies in healing. Moreover, I found that by the third session, the amount of relationship difficulties decreased as both partners became more aware of what their mates were experiencing, as they both felt more equipped to regulate or calm themselves, and as they both became more intentional in their actions.

This is the work—moving from survival mode into empowerment, from reacting to choosing, from conflict to connection. It's hard, it's messy, but it's the only way forward.

Let's go deeper.

QUESTION

How might your current behaviors be unintentionally reinforcing painful patterns in your relationships? Are there times when your need to protect yourself might be causing more harm than healing?

9

"You weren't emotionless. You were overtrained in silence. *But no one can love the version of you that never shows up."*

-Dr. Renee

The laugh was automatic, reflexive. It kept her from truly engaging with her pain and made her seem unfazed, even when she was crumbling inside.

Chapter Nine
Emotionless

Kayla was on her way to ending another relationship. "He cheated, and I'm done," she said matter-of-factly, a hollow laugh escaping her lips. Oddly, she continued to giggle as she recounted the story of how her boyfriend's other girlfriend had contacted her out of the blue. "She found me on Facebook, and we talked for hours," she said, as if it were the most casual conversation in the world.

Kayla was new to my office but not new to heartbreak. She was in her early fifties and looked like a model—poised, polished, and put-together. She exuded success, and her speech was articulate and precise. "This always happens to me. Every boyfriend or husband I've ever had has cheated on me," she said, almost as if she were sharing a trivial fact. It was fascinating because I could easily imagine men tripping over themselves to be with her. She had been married twice and divorced twice.

"I did everything right. I can't understand why," she said with a strained smile. There was that laugh again—slightly forced, slightly too loud. It seemed almost like a reflex, an automatic response that had nothing to do with humor or joy. "I'm successful. I made sure to offer sex to my husband as often as he wanted. I always carved out time to sit and listen about their day. I cooked and made sure we ate at the dinner table together. I'm that kind of girl who loves to watch sports and have a good time with my man," she said, listing out the qualities that, on paper, made her the perfect partner.

Kayla went on to describe how, after each relationship ended, she reached out to her exes—boyfriends, husbands—to ask why they had cheated on her. She detailed, almost clinically, the feedback they gave her. Each piece of input was noted and cataloged, as if she were building a case study.

"So, when you think about all the feedback you've gotten, what do you believe they were telling you?" I asked.

"I don't know!" she said, still giggling. But this time, I noticed the laughter was higher pitched, almost frantic. There was no humor in it. It was a defense mechanism, an automatic reaction. It was her newborn brain acting on autopilot, using that laughter to keep her away from her own emotions, from the core feelings buried deep within. The laughter created a distance between her and I—probably the same distance her partners felt. Her laughter could be easily perceived as heartless or cold, and it was important she understood this.

The Foundation Without the Glue

Kayla was an expert at building relationships—at least on a structural level. She created what looked like the perfect relationship on the outside: regular communication, shared interests, physical intimacy, and a commitment to quality time together. She'd mastered the art of creating a foundation and a structure. But what she didn't realize was that she was missing the most crucial component—the glue. Feelings and emotions, trust and vulnerability, the elements that bind a relationship and turn it from a structure into a living, breathing entity, were completely absent.

In our sessions, I began to understand that Kayla's automatic laughter and perfectly built relationships were a cover for her deep inability to connect emotionally—not only with her partners but also with herself. She had spent so much time avoiding her own feelings that she made no room for anyone else's, including her daughter's. She had been creating emotionally sterile environments, where the structure was solid but utterly devoid of life.

"Where are your emotions and feelings?" I asked her directly one day. She looked startled, the question catching her off guard. For the first time, she didn't laugh.

Kayla's Story: Childhood Conditioning

Kayla was an only child with an alcoholic mother. Her mother was young, overwhelmed, and utterly unprepared for parenthood. From a young age, Kayla had to take on the role of caregiver, becoming the responsible one in the household because her mother wasn't capable. She was the one who managed the household, paid the bills, and took care of her mother when she came home drunk. By high school, she was using her lunch breaks to catch the city bus and retrieve her mother's paycheck to ensure the rent was paid and the utilities stayed on.

Kayla became the adult, the foundation that kept everything from falling apart. Her mother praised her for being so mature, for keeping everything together. She was lauded for her responsibility but never allowed to be a child. Her mother's praise was the only form of acknowledgment she received, and it reinforced a dangerous narrative: **As long as you do everything perfectly and keep things running smoothly, you're doing your job.** As most children do, Kayla continued to give more of what she was rewarded for. She even started to accept it as a way of her mom showing her love.

Feelings? Emotions? They were irrelevant. They had no place

in the role Kayla was forced to play. And she internalized that lesson deeply. **Emotions didn't get bills paid**. Emotions didn't keep the lights on. **Emotions just got in the way**. So, she pushed them down, locked them away, and built her life on efficiency and structure instead.

The Automatic Reaction: Laughter

When her emotions did rise up—when something threatened to crack the shell of her perfection—her newborn brain reacted instinctively. It threw up a shield in the form of laughter. It was a way to deflect, to distract, to avoid facing the raw, painful feelings lurking just beneath the surface. The laugh was automatic, reflexive. It kept her from truly engaging with her pain and made her seem unfazed, even when she was crumbling inside.

But that same laughter, that same avoidance of feelings, meant she made no space for anyone else's emotions either. She couldn't handle her own, so how could she possibly make room for her partner's or her daughter's? Her relationships, no matter how well structured, always crumbled because there was no glue to hold them together.

Facing the Missing Pieces

The work with Kayla was painstaking. She had spent five decades perfecting the art of ignoring her emotions. When I asked her to describe how she felt, she stared at me blankly. "**I don't have any**," she said, the laughter gone now. She wasn't joking. She genuinely didn't know how to access her emotions.

"**I'm in my fifties, and I have no idea how to identify my feelings**," she admitted. For someone who had always prided herself on being so in control, it was a terrifying realization. The experiences from birth to twenty-five—her wild brain's most formative years—had conditioned her to create a system that worked, but it was a system that excluded the very thing that makes relationships thrive: **emotional connection**.

Identifying the Core Feelings

It took several sessions and the use of a feelings chart before Kayla could even begin to identify what she was feeling. When we finally started peeling back the layers, we found sadness.

"Since the last session, I've been able to identify that I feel sad most of the time. I just don't show it," she confessed. She was sad because she'd never been allowed to be a child. She was sad because she had spent her life trying to build relationships without ever allowing herself to fully engage in them.

"I looked at my daughter when she came over," she told me in a later session, "and I can see how my lack of emotions and feelings has impacted my daughter." For the first time, she was seeing how her emotional disconnect was affecting others. Her daughter, much like her, had learned to avoid her own feelings. Her daughter mirrored her, building structures without substance, foundations without glue.

Breaking the Cycle

With Kayla, the goal wasn't just to build the foundation of a good relationship model. It was to teach her how to add the missing glue—the feelings, the emotions, the trust and safety that make a relationship more than just a functional system. We explored the narratives in her wild brain that told her emotions were dangerous, that feeling made her weak, that if she let herself be vulnerable, everything would fall apart.

We talked about how her attempts to keep herself from feeling had also kept her from truly connecting. In avoiding her own emotions, she had created a wall that kept everyone at a distance. The laughter that had been her armor was also her prison, trapping her in a cycle of emotionally sterile relationships.

Moving Forward

Today, Kayla is still working to understand her feelings. She's learning to express sadness, anger, and even joy in ways that aren't masked by laughter. She's rebuilding her relationship with her daughter, making space for her daughter's emotions and her own. She's starting to see that, while structure is important, it's the emotional glue that holds everything together.

"You can build the most beautiful house," I told her in one session. "But without the glue, the walls won't hold. It will crumble under the slightest pressure."

Kayla nodded thoughtfully, her eyes misty but focused. *"I guess I've been building houses without glue my whole life," she said softly.*

"Yes," I said gently. "But now you know what's missing. And now you can change it."

Let's go deeper.

QUESTION

What emotions do you tend to avoid or suppress, and what automatic reactions do you use to hide them?

10

"You don't have a love problem. You have a trust problem. *And until you heal that, every relationship will feel like a gamble."*

-Dr. Renee

Behavior always follows belief. If you believe people will reject you, your brain will prepare for that loss before it even happens.

Chapter Ten

The Intellect

Though she was tall and striking; today, Tasha looked small—almost childlike. Tears slid down her cheeks as her voice cracked between frustration and sorrow.

"If I'm such a great catch, why do they always choose someone else?" she asked.

This wasn't just one or two men. According to Tasha, it was a pattern—a string of men who praised her, called her "wifey material," and then disappeared or chose someone else.

On paper, Tasha was everything people admired—a beautiful, well-respected African American woman with intelligence, poise, and presence. On stages, in boardrooms, and among her peers, she was celebrated for her brilliance and her ability to command a room. But here, in this room, her strength collapsed under the weight of her own thoughts—convinced she had somehow failed, yet again, to be chosen. "They always choose someone else," she whispered, almost to herself.

The silence was heavy. Her eyes met mine, wet and searching, as though I might finally hand her the missing piece.

I leaned forward in my chair. "Tasha, I see you've analyzed this situation enough to tell me what you think is happening, but can you give me a feeling? How does all of this make you feel?"

Her brain went into overdrive, scanning for the "right" answer. That was her pattern—placing intellect where her emotions should be. It was safer there, protected behind analysis and logic. But safety was costing her connection.

"There's no right or wrong answer here," I interrupted gently but firmly. "Get out of your head and into your body."

Her eyes dropped. Her body folded in on itself, smaller now, like disappearing would hurt less than being exposed. "I don't know how to explain it," she whispered, exhausted and defeated. She sank into her chair like air rushing out of a balloon.

The truth was clear: this wasn't just Tasha's intellect at work. This was her wild brain, doing what it had always done—convincing her that vulnerability wasn't safe, that emotions were dangerous, and that survival meant hiding behind her mind.

I waited a moment, then said quietly, locking eyes with her, "I don't need your analysis, Tasha; I need your feelings."

Tasha's Story: The Perfect Family

Tasha was raised in a family everyone admired. Her father was respected in the neighborhood, the kind of man people noticed when he entered a room. Tall, confident, and charismatic, he knew how to command attention and wore the appearance of stability like a tailored suit. Her mother played the part of composure. To outsiders, she looked like the well-protected wife—graceful, supportive, and perfectly aligned to make room for her husband's lead.

Tasha and her sister were polished extensions of the image, dressed neatly, well-spoken, and well-mannered. Neighbors praised them as the model family, the kind others tried to replicate.

Behind closed doors, the performance ended. The reality was wearing them all down like a heavy coat. The admiration from neighbors didn't erase the hurt, pain, and disappointment that hung in the air like a thick fog—a fog that no one dared to acknowledge. Every new pursuit meant the family would be moving. Although to the outside they were the model of stability, to Tasha and her family, stability only existed in their fantasies.

The father everyone admired for his strength and confidence was never satisfied. No matter what he achieved, it wasn't enough. He was always chasing the next best thing, convinced the next opportunity would finally fill the emptiness inside him. For Tasha's mother, it was exhausting. For Tasha and her sister, it was painful. Each move meant walking into another new school, starting over, and bracing for the sting of not being accepted—again.

Not Good Enough

Eventually, her father decided the best way to create "stability" was to leave his family with his parents while he chased the next dream. What he called stability was actually a nightmare. Instead of safety, they were met with rejection. It was made painfully clear—they weren't good enough to be accepted.

Tasha was impacted the most. Criticism and ridicule became routine. She walked away from every interaction feeling drained and worthless. The damage was sharp because, before moving in with her father's family, she had finally found a place where she belonged. In her old neighborhood, she had friends. She was known, celebrated for her brilliance, and she felt safe.

But at her grandparents' home, she was berated and unseen. Eventually, their criticism hardened into truth: She wasn't good enough. Worst of all, her father's version of "fixing it" left her unprotected, exposed, and on her own.

The Agreement

When home, her father overlooked his parents' misbehavior, and his silence made it clear he expected his family to do the same. His silence carried its own lesson: Emotions don't matter. Don't complain. Don't speak. Push forward. Tasha did just that. She continued to focus on her education, and she excelled. Constantly being awarded or acknowledged for her grades. Most of the time, he was consumed with his own search for meaning—except when Tasha excelled at school. He turned his full attention toward her then, doting on her achievements and bragging to anyone who would listen.

Without even knowing it, the agreement was made. To please him, Tasha stayed quiet, suppressed her feelings, and gave him what he wanted—her intellect.

When Silence Becomes Survival

Tasha's mother had learned to survive with her silence. She suppressed her pain, swallowed her anger, and never let her husband see how deeply she was suffering.

"Honey, he can't handle it if you told him how you really feel, so please don't," she would caution whenever Tasha thought about speaking up, about telling her father how much his absence hurt them.

The message etched itself into her nervous system. Her wild brain—built for survival—took that message and held it tight.

The Relational Template

"I'm not good enough. There is always a better option than me. My worth is my intellect. Stay silent in relationships even if you're hurt, in order to keep the peace." These weren't just random thoughts floating through Tasha's mind. They were conclusions built from experience—embedded over time, confirmed again and again until they became her truth. By adulthood, these beliefs were cemented in her wild brain.

That's how it works for all of us. The wild brain records what happens, stamps it as truth, and stores it away. Over time, those lessons become our relational template, the foundation for how we show up in nearly every relationship.

The danger is how sneaky this childhood baggage can be. Without realizing it, you start aligning your entire life around what you believe is true. And because most of us never pause long enough to check in, we don't challenge it—we just buy into it and start behaving.

You think you're responding to what's happening in the moment, but really, you're reacting to old wounds.

There are two truths to remember here.

<u>First:</u> **Behavior always follows belief**. If you believe people will reject you, your brain will prepare for that loss before it even happens. You'll scan every word, every gesture for proof that it's all falling apart. Once you're convinced you have identified evidence, you will show up with automatic behavior that, in essence, "protects" you but shuts others out. When others feel shut out, they just might pull away, and then you walk away feeling confirmed—*I knew I wasn't good enough*. In actuality, it happened

because you were afraid to let people get close enough to see that you were. Behavior follows belief, so always be willing to check in and see what your true beliefs are.

Second: **Healthy relationships require emotions**. If your partner or friend doesn't know how you feel, they have no compass. They have no idea how to maneuver the relationship with you, which makes it confusing and easy to disconnect. Or they might continue to show up with bad behavior because you have been unwilling to express how you feel. Yes, vulnerability is a risk, and we won't always know what's going to happen when we set boundaries or express ourselves in relationships, but what we do know is the lack of willingness only perpetuates more of what we don't want.

We unconsciously follow the rules of our relational template. For Tasha, that template meant entering relationships in survival mode. She was convinced she had to prove herself, hide herself, and mute herself.

Her intellect became armor—front and center to distract from the parts of herself she believed were unworthy. Overperforming, overproducing, and overengineering became her default. The problem wasn't her worth, it was her old, outdated template. She was still surviving an absent father, critical family members, and bullies at school. Her core beliefs were running in the background on repeat, keeping her locked in survival. All she could see was the narrative from the wild brain.

Eventually, Tasha was able to recognize this wasn't just about dating. She had carried the same template into many of her relationships—giving too much, staying too long, and holding onto connections that no longer served her.

Awareness: Dating, Marriage, and Connection

The work here is awareness. Without it, you'll confuse survival for love. The eight-year-old inside you is always craving what she didn't get and will do whatever it takes to finally have it. The adult may want something completely different, but if you don't stop and check in, it's easy to conflate the two—mistaking what the child wants for what the adult desires.

And when the eight-year-old wins, the adult pays. Maybe not immediately, but eventually you find yourself wondering, *How in the hell did I get here? What was I thinking?* The truth is, you weren't—the eight-year-old was driving. I see it all the time with clients who come to me exhausted, confused, wondering how they missed the signs. *It all started out so well... I don't know how I missed who they really were.* Put it this way: when the eight-year-old takes the wheel, you're bound to crash.

Who's really driving your relationships—the adult you or the eight-year-old still fighting old battles?

Here's the reality: You can be the best person in the world, but you don't experience yourself—others do. If what they encounter is your survival mode, your baggage spilling over, they may eventually leave. Not because you aren't good enough but because all that mess in the middle blocks them from seeing and connecting with the real you.

And this doesn't stop at dating. Many of you reading this are married right now, and the same applies. If you don't learn how to get your little person under control, your partner will be forced to calm it, parent it, and survive it—all at once. Love can make them willing, but it won't make them limitless. Over time, the weight will break them down.

This is why awareness of your cycle is non-negotiable. If you don't understand it, you'll miss the red flags every time. Think about it: If you grew up with a mother who was selfish or narcissistic, you probably learned early that love was conditional. Maybe she pulled away when she didn't get what she wanted, and you had to "fix it" to earn her attention back. Over time, that became training. Without realizing it, you built a relational template: love is something I have to earn; love is something I have to repair.

When you date with "fix-it" energy, you teach others you'll carry the blame and smooth things over—no matter what. And if you've never experienced unconditional love, trusting it feels almost impossible. Your wild brain may even see it as a threat. Instead of receiving genuine care, you push it away and cling to what feels familiar—conditional love, the only version you know.

That's why unhealthy behaviors don't always look like red flags. They feel like home. And before you know it, you're back in the same cycle, trying to fix your way into love.

How many times have you mistaken familiarity for love simply because it felt like home?

Awareness exposes the wound, but awareness alone won't heal it. You must anchor yourself in something stronger, something that pulls you out of the grip of that child self. That's where the irrefutable truth comes in. It is the only thing strong enough to silence the wild brain and put the eight-year-old back to bed.

Getting Out of Your Wounds and into Your Wisdom: The Irrefutable Truth

After helping Tasha understand her cycles, the most powerful shift came when she discovered her irrefutable truth. She had been so lost in old stories that she couldn't even hear what her friends had been telling her for years.

"Almost every year, my friends celebrate my birthday with a dinner," she told me during one session. "At some point, they all take turns telling me how much I am loved, admired, and necessary in their lives." She paused, shaking her head in disbelief. "This is the first year I feel like I actually heard them."

That's the power of the wild brain—it hijacks you from the truth that has been right in front of you all along. It took time, but Tasha was able to see it: When she showed up whole, her relationships were solid. The truth had always been the truth—she was loved, admired, and necessary to many people.

The only way to combat the wild brain's stories is to anchor yourself in the irrefutable truth. The irrefutable isn't something you make up to feel better. It's not positive thinking. It's not even your feelings—because feelings can lie. The irrefutable is what has already been proven to you over and over again. It cannot be changed. It is not up for debate. It is fact.

For Tasha, the irrefutable truth was this: No one had ever told her she wasn't good enough. Year after year, her friends told her the opposite—that she was amazing, relevant, and necessary. Awareness was the missing piece. The eight-year-old wanted to be chosen, when the adult had already been chosen all along. Remember this: The wild brain holds the narratives. The observer brain holds the truth.

Once Tasha began to recognize her irrefutable truth, she anchored herself in it. So, when the wild brain tried to drag her back into the story of rejection and abandonment, she could stop the spiral by holding onto what had already been proven—that she had always been loved and accepted, simply for being her.

And that's the lesson for all of us: Survival will never set you free. **Only the truth can do that.**

The Road to Change

Today, Tasha no longer shrinks back or hides behind her intellect. She leans into hard conversations with clarity and confidence—and even welcomes them. One of the hardest choices she's made was ending a long-term relationship she once feared leaving, after realizing it survived only on her silence and self-sacrifice—the very patterns of her outdated relational template.

She's challenging her family to discuss issues more openly and honestly. "My mom didn't want to say anything to my dad the other day," she told me in session. "She asked me not to say anything either."

"Oh yeah? And what did you do?" I asked, curious to see how she handled the situation.

"I told her, 'I understand if *you* don't want to say anything, but *my* feelings are involved too. So, *I will* be talking to him about how his actions made *me* feel.'"

I was proud of her. She was finally willing to take the risk and use her voice. Her voice didn't shake. She was confident, direct, unwavering.

"Tasha," I said, setting my pen down, "I hope you see it now—

you never had a man problem. You had a trust problem. You didn't trust you were enough. You didn't trust what was happening in the present. You didn't trust yourself." I paused. "But now you do. And I can see it."

That's the real breakthrough. Not just finding her voice—but trusting it.

QUESTION

Are you using intellect, achievements, or perfectionism to avoid feeling vulnerable? What emotions might be hiding beneath your desire to appear 'strong' or 'put-together'?

11

You've done "strong." You've done "silent." You've done "fix it."

Now it's time to do honest. Because that's where freedom lives.

-Dr. Renee

Let's face it, embrace it, and replace it—so you can finally get out of your wounds and into wisdom. You deserve it.

Chapter Eleven

Own It

This book isn't about giving you new ideas or revolutionary techniques. It's not here to introduce fancy terminology or groundbreaking theories. Instead, it's about something much simpler and far more important: getting to the truth of why you keep ending up in the same painful patterns, why you feel stuck, and why—no matter how much you try—you can't seem to break free from the baggage you've been dragging around for years.

What I've done is take concepts we're all familiar with—concepts like emotional baggage, destructive cycles, and self-sabotage—and go deeper. I've put the meat on the bone, offering a clear, practical framework so you can finally understand what's really going on and do something about it.

From Gale, who was overlooked because she shrunk herself, to Dave, whose wild brain sent him into emotional warfare, to Sophie and Dewayne, whose pain created a toxic dance that left them both wounded—we've explored story after story, each one showing you a different facet of how your brain, your emotions, and your past experiences shape the way you respond to life.

These stories aren't just about other people. They're about you.

Whether you're single, dating, married, or trying to navigate a career, at least one of these stories should have hit close to home.

And that's the point. Because the goal of this book is for you to see yourself more clearly, to identify your own cycles, and, ultimately, to own your sh!t.

Seeing the Patterns in Yourself

When I say "own your sh!t," I mean something very specific. I'm talking about looking at the patterns that keep you stuck and naming them for what they are. I'm talking about stepping back from your knee-jerk reactions, your emotional triggers, and your old wounds to see them clearly: the past replaying itself over and over again, hijacking your present. This book isn't a replacement for therapy, but it is a powerful guide to help you break the cycle and move forward with a new level of awareness.

Let's recap the core concepts:

The Three Brains: The Drivers Behind Your Behavior

You've learned that your brain isn't a single unit but a complex system with three distinct parts.

1. **The Newborn Brain** – The oldest, most primitive part of your brain. It's automatic and reactive, triggering fight, flight, freeze, or fawn behaviors. It doesn't think or plan—it just responds. This is where those gut reactions come from, where you find yourself doing something before you even realize what's happening.
2. **The Wild Brain** – The midbrain, which stores the most emotionally intense and painful memories, rejection, and fear you've experienced. This is the source of those internal narratives—the voices that say, "You're not good enough,"

"You're going to be abandoned," or "You'll never be safe." When your Wild Brain is activated, your Observer Brain—the rational, truth-seeking part of your mind—gets shut down. The newborn brain and the midbrain combined make up your emotional brain.

3. **The Observer Brain** – The adult, rational brain that sees things clearly, processes logically, and tells you the truth. This is the part of your brain that can break through the Wild Brain's distortions and ground you in reality. But accessing it takes effort. It requires pausing, stepping back, and bringing yourself back to the present moment.

The OWN Method: Observing What's Happening Now

The *OWN Method* is a tool to help you bring your Observer Brain online when you're triggered. The acronym stands for *Observe What's Happening Now*:

1. Observe what's happening in your mind and body.
2. Identify which brain is in control—Newborn Brain, Wild Brain, or Observer Brain.
3. Pause before you act, and make a conscious decision to choose a new response.

The OWN Method is about awareness. It's about recognizing when your Newborn or Wild Brain is running the show, and choosing to step into your Observer Brain instead. It's the first step in breaking the automatic cycles that have kept you stuck.

The Feelings Cycle: Understanding Your Emotional Triggers

The *Feelings Cycle* helps you see the pattern beneath the pattern. When you're triggered, it starts with a feeling, which then creates a thought, which leads to an action. Breaking it down like this allows you to see exactly what's happening in your body and mind when you're caught in a cycle:

1. **What do I feel?**
2. **What are my thoughts?**
3. **What are my typical actions or reactions?**

Mapping out your Feelings Cycle shows you the core feelings that are driving your behavior. Maybe it's fear. Maybe it's shame. Maybe it's loneliness. Whatever it is, naming it is the first step toward changing it.

The Power Cycle: Anchoring Yourself in Truth

Once you've identified your destructive cycle, the next step is shifting into the *Power Cycle*. This is about grounding yourself in the truth, using your Observer Brain to access what's real, and choosing to respond from a place of strength and clarity:

1. **What do I know for sure?**
2. **What is the irrefutable truth about me?**
3. **What will I choose to do differently?**

The Power Cycle is where transformation happens. It's where you shift from reacting based on old pain to responding based on what's real. It's about breaking free from the Wild Brain's stories and stepping into your own power.

A Framework for Breaking the Cycle

If you've been following along with the workbook, you should now have a clear picture of your own cycles—the old narratives stored in your Wild Brain, the automatic behaviors driven by your Newborn Brain, and the truth that only your Observer Brain can see. You should know what's been keeping you stuck, and you should have a framework for how to break those patterns:

1. **Identify the Feelings Cycle**: Map out your emotional triggers and automatic reactions.
2. **Shift into the Power Cycle**: Ground yourself in the truth and choose a new response.
3. **Use the OWN Method**: Observe what's happening now and consciously choose which brain to let drive your behavior.

Your Own Story

This book isn't just a guide. It's a mirror. If you found yourself in any of the stories I shared—whether it was Gale's need to stay invisible, Dave's knee-jerk defensiveness, Sophie's flight responses, or Dewayne's rage—you're not alone. Every one of us are walking around with invisible baggage, playing out old patterns from childhood. But by following this framework, you can break free.

The Road Ahead

This book doesn't promise instant change. Breaking these patterns is hard work. It requires dedication, self-reflection, and a willingness to sit with your own pain. But it's possible. The more you practice the OWN Method, the more you map out your Feelings Cycle and shift into the Power Cycle, the stronger your Observer Brain becomes. And when your Observer Brain is running the show, you're no longer at the mercy of your Wild Brain's distortions or your Newborn Brain's automatic behaviors.

Final Words

Whatever you refuse to own will eventually own you. Your history is etched in your mind, stored in your Wild Brain, driving your behavior every single day. But now, you have a choice. You have a framework. You know what to look for, what to ask, and how to respond. You know how to OWN your sh!t.

So, if you've been living in the same destructive cycles, trapped by the same triggers, take a breath. You've already taken the hardest step—becoming aware of the cycle. From here, it's about making new choices one day at a time until those new choices become the new normal.

And if there's one thing, I want you to remember from this book, it's this: **Whatever you refuse to own will own you.**

Take your power back. No more charging others with the responsibility of managing your sh!t. Let's face it, embrace it, and replace it—so you can finally get out of your wounds and into wisdom. You deserve it.

Observe

What's (happening)

Now (with the)

Stuff

Hijacking (you from the)

Irrefutable

Truth

www.ingramcontent.com/pod-product-compliance
Lightning Source LLC
LaVergne TN
LVHW100320210926
848480LV00003B/1198